Politics of Fear

Related titles:

Culture of Fear (revised edition), Frank Furedi

Where Have All the Intellectuals Gone?, Frank Furedi

Politics of **Fear**

Frank Furedi

continuum

Continuum International Publishing Group
The Tower Building
11 York Road
London SE1 7NX

15 East 26th Street
New York
NY 10010

www.continuumbooks.com

British Library Cataloguing-in-Publication Data
A catalogue record for this book is available from the British Library.

ISBN: 0-8264-8728 9 (hardback)

Typeset by BookEns Ltd, Royston, Herts.
Printed and bound in Great Britain by MPG Books Ltd, Bodmin, Cornwall

Contents

Foreword

*Do you begin to see then, what kind of world we are creating?
It is the exact opposite of the stupid hedonistic Utopias that
the old reformers imagined. A world of fear and treachery and
torment, a world of trampling and being trampled upon, a
world which will grow not less but more merciless as it refines
itself.*

George Orwell, *Nineteen Eighty-Four*

The politics of fear appears to dominate public life in Western
societies. We have become very good at scaring one another and
appearing scared. These days we indicate our disagreement with
a public figure by announcing to the world that we find him or
her frightening. 'I find Bush really scary' or 'I am really frightened
of what Blair is likely to do' is another way of saying that I dislike
their views. From the food we consume to our anxieties about
children, being scared has become a culturally sanctioned
affectation that pervades all aspect of life. Yet too often we tend
to trivialize the dimension of this phenomenon. Commentators
often blame a particular politician or party for 'practising' the
politics of fear. Unfortunately this practice is not restricted to a
particular party. As I argue in this book the practice has been
internalized by the entire political class and has become
institutionalized in public life.

The politics of fear is symptomatic of the pervasive sense of
exhaustion and disengagement that affects public life. Public life
in general and politics in particular is in danger of losing its sense

of meaning and purpose. It is easy to overlook the fact that this is
not simply a problem for the professional politician. Cynicism
and suspicion towards politics ultimately represents cynicism and
suspicion towards one another. Statements like 'I don't trust
politicians' or 'I don't believe what they say' simply rationalize
the retreat from public life. They convey a profound sense of
fatalism and suggest that politics is a pointless exercise. These
sentiments are not the inevitable response to the misdeed of
public figures. In previous times people have reacted to politicians
whom they did not trust by getting rid of them or by even trying
to change the system. Today people are more likely to react by
switching off and disengaging from public life. That is what
happened during the 2005 General Election in Britain, even
though the turnout for this was slightly higher than for that in
2001. Politicians and commentators continually alluded to the
politics of fear. And people nodded before they nodded off to
sleep.

If politics is indeed pointless then we are quite entitled to fear
everything. In modern times politics provided the promise of
people being able to exercise a degree of control over their
destiny. Since the Enlightenment of the eighteenth century, it was
associated with the project of conquering Fate. One important
legacy of this process was that humanity was less prepared to
accept an externally imposed destiny. People became less
disposed to accept disease and death. Fewer men and women
were prepared to accept acts of misfortune as the will of God.
And more and more came to believe that their lives could be
altered and improved. Politics was embraced because it offered
the promise of choice and alternative paths to the future.

Thankfully most of us are still not inclined to accept our fate.
People spend billions on health care, attempt to slow down the
process of ageing, and even alter the way they look. Some travel
hundreds or thousands of miles in search of a new life. But while
we attempt to gain a measure of control over the direction of our

individual circumstances, we find it difficult to give direction to public affairs. Rather a sense of political exhaustion seems to govern public affairs. The clearest manifestation of this trend is the tendency to see people as the object rather than agent of change. This book looks at the way the exhaustion of public life is paralleled by the decline of the Enlightenment ideal of personhood and argues that the interaction between the two provides the dynamic for the politics of fear.

The aim of this book is not simply to discuss a serious problem facing society but to confront the predominant way that it is interpreted. There appears to be a refusal to accept and engage with the problems thrown up by the prevailing regime of political and social disengagement. Indeed, there is a discernible tendency to deny the existence of the problem and even to create the impression that what we are going through is merely a more mature and democratic political era. Despite what we often intuitively grasp we find it difficult to acknowledge the appalling state of public life. Many commentators reject the idea that apathy is a problem. They desperately attempt to invent or discover new forms of activism, new politics or new social movements. They continually expand the meaning of participation so that membership of an Internet chat group, a patient self-help group or the signing of a petition is represented as the manifestation of the highest civic virtue. In this book, this response is characterized as *politics in denial*. Politics in denial can be understood in two different senses. It first of all denies the relevance of politics and claims that we live in a world where there is little scope for political action. But secondly, it denies the reality of a deeply entrenched mood of political disengagement. I believe that this sense of complacency and conformism transmitted by sections of the political elite contributes to making the situation worse.

However, the world is not all gloom and doom. Despite a growing momentum of cultural fatalism and political illiteracy humanity consistently demonstrates that it is capable of great achievements. It is difficult to be pessimistic about the future as long as people continue to demonstrate their aspiration to make things happen. This book argues that the antidote to fatalism is the perspective of humanizing humanism. The way to confront the prevailing culture of fatalism is by rescuing the legacy of the humanist Enlightenment and humanizing it further. In particular, we need to develop a more challenging narrative of personhood than the current feeble version.

The exhaustion of public life also calls into question the relevance of many of the principal political categories of modern times. This book argues that concepts like left and right have little content and their usage has mainly a rhetorical character. In our pre-political era what matters today is the role we assign to humanity and to the individual. Fundamental ideas about personhood shape attitudes towards change and the direction of the future. Today a progressive outlook needs to adopt a positive outlook towards individual autonomy, the exercise of freedom, risk taking and scientific and social experimentation. It needs to uphold the achievements of human civilization in the past and adopt an open-ended orientation towards the future. Such a perspective, which amounts to the rejection of fate, represents the negation of the politics of fear.

Lots of people helped me work out the ideas for this book. Josie Appleton, Sabine Reul, Helen Searls and Mick Hume continually fed me lots of interesting material; Tracey Brown's comments on an early draft helped me to focus some of the arguments; and, from its inception, Anthony Haynes, my editor at Continuum, was hugely supportive of the project. My thanks to them all.

1   Politics is Lost for Words

Politics is lost for words. Public figures find it difficult to account for their concerns in the language of politics. Instead of addressing people about their beliefs, principles or doctrines they modestly refer to an 'agenda' or a 'project'. Speech writers and spin doctors often brainstorm to come up with what George Bush tried to describe as 'the vision thing' and are continually on the prowl for the 'Big Idea'. But unfortunately for them, political life has turned into a vision-free zone. It is a sign of the times that politicians have become attached to the term 'vision thing'. Even opponents of Bush no longer scorn this term as the product of an intellectually lightweight imagination. Since November 2004, numerous Democracts have blamed their defeat on the absence of the 'vision thing'.

George Orwell in his famous 1946 essay 'Politics and the English Language' was intensely concerned about the decline of the standard of political rhetoric in his time. He was also perturbed by the way jargon was used to obscure reality. 'In our time, political speech and writing are largely the defence of the indefensible,' observed Orwell. He noted how policies like British rule of India, the Stalinist purges or the dropping of the atom bomb on Hiroshima were justified through euphemisms and meaningless phraseology. No doubt, political rhetoric today continues to justify the indefensible. Terms like 'empowerment' and 'support' invariably represent an invitation to bureaucratic intrusion. The word 'choice', especially when associated with health and education, tends to signify the absence of alternatives.

The phrase 'collateral damage' serves to distract attention from the brutal consequences of warfare on the civilian population. In Iraq people are degraded rather than killed. But the defence of the indefensible is by no means the distinctive feature of the contemporary political vocabulary. Today, politics seems pre-occupied with justifying its very existence. And the rhetoric that politicians adopt is just that – rhetoric. Even some of the most widely used slogans and terms turn out to be words in search of meaning.

It is difficult to avoid the impression that a key function of today's political vocabulary is to distract attention from the underlying dearth of ideas. Its role is to provide public figures with the breathing space to figure out what to say next. Behind the words lurks the hope that they might provide the spark for a new idea. Take the concept of the Third Way. No doubt it must mean something very important. Otherwise why have there been so many debates and conferences dedicated to the discovery of just what is meant by New Labour's Third Way? There is a veritable literature devoted to deciphering the meaning of this term. Many political scientists still find it difficult to consider the possibility that the Third Way actually means very little, and that there is very little to discover about its hidden meaning. Shouting out that the Emperor has no clothes is often difficult for academics engaged in the analysis of concepts. Nevertheless, for some the penny has dropped. According to one account there is no 'big idea' behind the term or rather, 'the big idea is that there is no big idea'.[1] Is it possible that when Britain's Deputy Prime Minister John Prescott asserts that 'the whole philosophy of our approach is to strengthen local responsibility and to have a bottom-up approach' he has only verbiage but not ideas to communicate? Or do we need to organize a series of workshops to deconstruct the meaning of a 'bottom-up approach'?

Increasingly the rhetoric adopted by the political elites is deployed to obscure the fact that, not only do they not have a big idea, but they also lack even a small one. Occasionally a politician breaks ranks and publicly decries the vacuous character of contemporary public discourse. Just before Christmas 2004, Tessa Jowell, the Culture Secretary in Britain's New Labour Government, stated that at meetings she makes notes on the 'absurd language we use' and files these in her 'little book of bollocks'. The kind of politician's gobbledegook she had in mind were terms like 'reprofiling expenditure', 'sustainable eating in schools'; 'regional cultural data feedback roll-out' or 'strategic objectives for evaluation'.[2]

Of course it is difficult not to ridicule the Orwellian-sounding managerial jargon that pervades political debate on both sides of the Atlantic. However, politicians like Jowell still find it difficult to acknowledge the fact that the use of jargon has become the norm. Indeed most of the fashionable political terms used by her and her colleagues in government also lack precision and substance. Take some of the Hurrah Words that trip off the tongue of public figures. Everybody is for diversity, transparency, social cohesion, inclusion, best practice, adding value, stakeholding or sustainability. But what do these words mean? When a term like sustainable is used as an adjective to qualify nouns like development, targets, partnership, community, funding, strategy or education, it is evident that its purpose is simply to signal approval. It appears that sustainable is good because clearly anything that is unsustainable is bad. So when politicians are lost for words their instinct is to shout 'sustainable something'.

The embrace of empty phraseology is not confined to the political Establishment but extends also to many of its critics. Since the publication of Hardt and Negri's *Empire*, the term Empire has become an all-purpose concept attached to forces and institutions that radical critics find objectionable. But what is this Empire that does not even need a definite article to pin down its meaning? According to its authors 'it is a *decentered* and *deterritorializing* apparatus of rule that progressively incorporates the entire global realm within its open, expanding frontiers'. It is here, there and everywhere and in case you are still confused, the authors are happy to elaborate its meaning: 'Empire manages hybrid identities, flexible hierarchies, and plural exchanges through modulating networks of command.'[3] This 'subversive' phraseology promoted by radical critics dominated by a postmodern imagination is the flip-side of the managerial gobbledegook of the Western political class. Their depoliticized language reflects a profound sense of estrangement from the world of politics as it is classically understood.

The impoverishment of the language of public life, or what the Australian social critic Don Watson describes as the 'decay of public language', suggests that when it comes to politics we are unable to find the right words. Commentators still talk about parties, but most people in the know comprehend that these outfits bear little resemblance to the organizations that dominated the political landscape of the previous century. Hardly anybody is a member of a party. Many of this dying breed are 'sleeping members', not even aware of their membership, and even more are entirely inactive. Television producers often face difficulties when transmitting images of party conferences and meetings. The empty seats and the mood of tedium and boredom that dominates these events gives the proceedings an artificiality that makes for bad television. Is it any surprise that mass political parties with long historical traditions – Progressive Conservatives in Canada, Christian Democrats in Italy – can literarily disappear?

It is difficult for activists to accept that their organization has turned into a party of courtiers and careerists. 'Is the Party Over?' asks the author of a Fabian Society pamphlet in its title. But despite all the damning evidence, he still clutches at the straws of hope. It appears that local Labour parties can be revived through putting the 'social' back into Socialism through giving their members a good social life.[4]

The irrelevance of the political vocabulary of the past two centuries is most striking when it comes to the traditional distinction between left and right. There was a time when these labels signified an important distinction between progressives and reactionaries. To put it crudely, the left wanted social change and looked forward to human emancipation. In contrast, the right dreaded change and robustly sought to uphold what it considered to be the traditional way of doing things. Today, people who regard themselves as right wing – and there are very few of them – have more or less given up on defending tradition. Episodic initiatives by conservatism to 'go back to basics' quickly give way to a mood of pragmatic compromise. Periodic attempts which aim to relaunch the conservative project often conclude with a plea for getting rid of the old ideological baggage. One recent well-argued case for rescuing conservatism suggests that this movement 'should be prepared to base itself on as few and as uncontroversial assumptions as could bear its weight'.[5] In the US 'compassionate conservatism' plays a role analogous to New Labour's Third Way. Even the so-called Religious Right, which is frequently presented as a dogmatic fundamentalist force, is in reality less in the business of defending old traditions than in inventing new ones. Promoting abstinence or intelligent design represents a rearguard action against an unpredictable world.

In March 2005 it was reported that the British Conservative Party was hoping to convince the media to stop calling its members Tories. It appears that throwing out four centuries of tradition is a small price to pay for appearing modern. Tradition is in retreat on every front. Fox hunters, public schools and elite universities protest that they are misunderstood, and that they are actually quite modern and normal. Rural Britain has responded to the attacks on its traditions not by upholding its right to age-old rituals but by arguing that hunting with dogs is an effective form of pest control. Even the churches cannot make up their minds about fundamental issues to do with doctrine and ritual.

Hesitancy and confusion tends to favour the modernizers in their battles with the ever-retreating traditionalists.

Just as the right no longer defends tradition, the left no longer embraces change. Those who call themselves left wing are among the most vociferous opponents of change today. Belief in the possibility of progress is already feeble within the societies of the twenty-first century. But probably its most fervent critics are to be found on the cultural left. The label 'progressive' ill fits a movement that is intensely suspicious of science and experimentation and regards new technology with dread. There was a time when left-wing thinkers took pride in the battle against all forms of superstition. Today's self-styled left embodies a hi-tech superstition that uses the Internet to spread rumours about risks and conspiracies linked to new technology. Often the difference that appears to divide the left from the right is focused on which innovation they wish to ban. For example, sections of the right would like to ban stem-cell research while many on the left want to rid the world of genetically modified products.

It is difficult to avoid the conclusion that the vocabulary of politics reflects a profound sense of confusion about how to approach the future. Society is uncomfortable with itself and invariably experiences change as a destructive process. At the same time society feels estranged from its past, unsure of what to uphold or retain. These sentiments are transmitted through a culture that endorses scepticism, relativism, cynicism – prime virtues of an outlook that prides itself on its detachment and lack of commitment. The political expression of this culture is an incoherent doctrine that can be termed the *conservatism of fear*.

The conservatism of fear has little in common with its classical counterpart. Whatever one thinks of classical conservatism, it at least possessed a belief in the unique character of a human being. In contrast, the conservatism of fear is driven by a profound misanthropic impulse. Moreover, unlike the old conservatism, it has no tradition to defend. Shared by former left and right alike, it is an outlook that is ill at ease with strongly held beliefs and values. None of its causes is sacred and it is always prepared to 'modernize' and 'compromise'. The conservatism of fear has lost its anchor in the past. The traditionalist aspiration for continuity has given way to a new, more relativist outlook, most frequently articulated by those not traditionally associated with the forces of the right. The most coherent exponents of the conservatism of fear are to be found amongst the ranks of people who were out protesting 'against capitalism' on the streets of Seattle, Genoa, Quebec City and London. Edmund Burke would have felt more comfortable than Thomas Paine or Karl Marx with the speeches given at Porto Alegre and at other meetings of the anti-capitalist World Social Forums. Yes, they are radical, but theirs is a radicalism oriented entirely against change. It is the fear of the future and of the consequences of change that shapes the imagination of this movement. The ethos of sustainability, the dogma of the precautionary principle, the idealization of nature, of the 'organic', all express a misanthropic mistrust of human ambition and experimentation. The anti-capitalism of the protestors on the streets of Seattle and London represented not the old dream of human liberation, but a fear of the future and a determination to seek refuge in a static predictable existence. At least intellectually, these anti-capitalists feel more at ease with the lifestyle that prevailed in the days when people lived in static rural communities, dominated by nature.

Politics will remain in a state of stasis as long as society feels so ill-prepared to manage change, because this kind of estrangement from the future undermines the capacity to generate ideas about what needs to be done. Without such ideas there can be no vision of the way ahead and no real choices to be made. But politics needs a future-oriented perspective and choice. At the very least politics has to offer a choice between leaving things the way they are or offering an alternative way of improving on the present. Without such an alternative what we are left with is a parody of

politics. As we shall see, it is the denial of human choice that fuels
the phenomenon that is increasingly characterized as the *politics
of fear*.

Is there really no alternative?

Perry Anderson, one of Britain's leading leftist intellectuals,
argues, 'for the first time since the reformation, there are no
longer any significant oppositions – that is systematic rival
outlooks'.[6] At election times political analysts make desperate
attempts to discover a hint of an ideological difference between
the candidates. But in the end, what really distinguishes a Bush
from a Kerry or a Blair from a Howard are matters of style and
personality traits. In Britain the attempt to endow the Blair–
Brown personality clash with ideological substance invariably
fails to persuade.

The erosion of the distinction between left and right and the
decline of the contestation of alternatives is frequently attributed
to the triumph of 'neo-liberalism'. 'Whatever limitations persist
to its practice, neo-liberalism as a set of principles rules undivided
across the globe: the most successful ideology in world history,'
argues Anderson. The claim that the triumph of neo-liberalism
has dealt a death-blow to political contestation has been argued
most forcefully by Francis Fukuyama. In an article published in
the *National Interest* in 1989, Fukuyama claimed that the
'unabashed victory of economic and political liberalism' has led
to the 'triumph of the West, of the Western *idea*'. He noted that
the fact that this was evident was demonstrated by the 'total
exhaustion of viable systematic alternatives to western liberalism'.[7] At first sight, Fukuyama's bold assertion that ideological
struggle and history have come to an end appears plausible.
However, as we shall see, the reality of political exhaustion
should not be confused with the ideological or intellectual

triumph of a particular way of life. Despite its victory over the bureaucratic regimes of the Eastern Bloc, liberal capitalism does not enjoy widespread intellectual or cultural support. Indeed, what is so striking in retrospect is just how swiftly the triumphalist phase of neo-liberalism came to an end. At a time when so many themes associated with anti-capitalism – corrupt corporates, greedy brand names, unfair trade deals – resonate with popular culture, it is difficult to find enthusiastic intellectual support for neo-liberalism.

It seems there is a mood of unprecedented intellectual diffidence and self-doubt amongst supporters of capitalism. Instead of a robust defence of enterprise or risk taking, company executives are more likely to hold forth about business ethics and responsibility to the community. The response of Starbucks to becoming the focus of anti-globalization protests is typical in this respect. Starbucks seeks to reinvent itself as an 'ethically responsible' firm – more a charity than a business.[8] At international conferences, so-called neo-liberals are conspicuously silent and defensive. After the 2005 World Economic Forum, Sir Digby Jones, Director General of the Confederation of British Industry, could not refrain from expressing his frustration at the defensive behaviour of his colleagues. He stated that he was 'worried and frustrated by the lack of celebration of risk takers and wealth creators' and unhappy with the way business people caved in to those 'who want business to apologise for itself'.[9] It is not triumphalism but a sense of disorientation that characterizes the mood of the advocates of enterprise.

Insofar as neo-liberalism ever appears triumphant it is only in contrast to the decline and disintegration of left-wing alternatives. Since the 1980s the political class has adopted the view that economic realities will always overwhelm political ambition. Clinton's banal statement 'it's the economy, stupid' has acquired the status of an unquestioned political truth. Political parties in and out of government have accommodated to this approach and

have adopted the view that the state is a relatively feeble
institution for dealing with the problems of society. This loss of
belief in the efficacy of the state and of government policy reflects
a general sense of disenchantment with politics. The Thatcherite
dictum 'There Is No Alternative' (TINA) clearly captured the
spirit of the eighties. It also represented a statement decrying the
futility of the political imagination. For if indeed there is no
alternative, politics can have little meaning. At best politics can
mean no more than fiddling around with minor issues on the
margins of society.

Some supporters of TINA attempt to present their case as if it
were based on some law of nature. Others account for their
adherence to TINA by arguing that material reality or conditions
of life have reached a stage where there is diminished scope for
political life. For example, it is frequently suggested that the
process of globalization has reduced the capacity of the nation
state to manage its affairs. Politicians and governments have been
quick to acquiesce to this outlook. 'Partly in recognition of this
new environment, governments in contemporary democracies
appear also increasingly keen to play down any "direct hands on"
responsibility, seeing their role instead as being that of a
facilitator rather than a manager,' notes one commentator.[10]
This new style of self-limitation clearly informs the perspective of
the Third Way. Advocates of the Third Way justify the modest
political role assigned to the state on the ground that there is no
alternative to the dynamic of globalization. They assert that the
imperative of economic competition forces all governments to
adopt similar policies. As a result, policies are no longer the
outcome of informed political debate but measures forced upon
governments by global forces that are beyond anyone's control.

But just what does TINA mean? It seems that this dictum can
be understood in at least two different senses. It is generally
understood as an expression of realism about the decisive
importance of the market on everyday life. From this standpoint

TINA represents the claim that there is no alternative to capitalism and to the operation of the free market and therefore the scope for state intervention is a relatively modest one. Whatever the merits of this claim, it is worth noting that neither of its principal proponents in the eighties – Reagan or Thatcher – actually acted according to its dictates. Neither succeeded in realizing their stated ambition of 'rolling back the state'. Indeed, during the Reagan-Thatcher years state expenditure continued to increase. Even these most fervent advocates of TINA must have noticed that there was an alternative to what they set out to achieve.

Another way of understanding TINA is that the statement reflects the *exhaustion of the political imagination*. In other words there is no alternative because we cannot think of one. Take the way the *Sun*, Britain's largest-selling daily newspaper, expresses this issue. At the start of the 2003 Labour Party Conference, this tabloid published a long editorial attacking the Blair Government's record in office. Nevertheless, it concluded the attack with the unexpected statement, 'we still back him'. Why? 'Increasingly, it feels as if we give him our support because there's no alternative,' it noted with an air of resignation.

The most useful way of understanding TINA is not as a statement that expresses the logic of global market forces but one that both reflects and promotes the prevailing sensibility of limits. This sensibility is by no means confined to discussions about the scope for policy making in the sphere of economics. Discussions about the big issues of the day appear to be dominated by a debilitating dogma of limits. Whether the controversy is about the economy, the environment, health care, science or social policy, there is an assumption that society is no longer capable of making much progress towards improving the human condition. Indeed it is often assumed that every attempt to change things is likely to make matters worse, since it will only throw up new problems and create risks to health, safety and the environment.

There is a widespread acceptance of the sentiment that we cannot overcome 'the environmental crisis' or the 'crisis of community' through conventional economic or social policies. We are continually told that there is no 'magic bullet' that can cure a specific disease. As for the next terrorist-induced catastrophe, the question is not whether it will happen but when. We are frequently informed that human action actually creates conditions that compromise the survival of the planet. It seems that humanity is the problem rather than the solution. The silver lining to this outlook is, I contend, that the notion that there is no alternative and that it is not really possible to solve most of the problems facing humanity is based not on an identification of new and insuperable difficulties, but on a novel underestimation of human capabilities. So while this prejudice is profoundly entrenched it can be contested.

Driven by the conservatism of fear, TINA is informed by a disturbingly pessimistic account of human limits. As I argue in Chapter 4, the last two decades have seen a radical reinterpretation of the meaning of personhood. This coincides with a constant inflation of the danger and problems which people face today, coupled with a lack of belief in humanity having the ability to tackle any difficulties we might come up against in the process. Such a pessimistic account of personhood renders political criticism and questioning entirely ineffectual. Indeed, as I shall argue, what's different today is not the number of problems we face, nor the scale of the dangers confronting us. It is the fatalistic spirit with which they are approached. The principal achievement of this fatalism is the normalization of the idea of 'not if ... but when'. So we take in our stride the announcement that 'ministers are preparing for a flu pandemic that they believe poses a far greater risk to Britons than a terrorist attack'.[11] The very same day as this warning is issued, we are also told that 'the world may have little more than a decade to avert catastrophic climate change'.[12] As the late Susan Sontag wrote so eloquently, 'that even an apocalypse can be made to seem part of the ordinary horizon of expectation constitutes an unparalleled violence that is being done to our sense of reality, to our humanity'.[13]

The culture of limits is now accepted as gospel by those who would see themselves on the left and the right alike. Critics and supporters of capitalism unite in insisting that there is little scope for effective political action. We are told that there is no alternative but to subordinate social objectives to the dictates of the free market, or that there is no alternative but to cut down on the consumption of resources to avert climate change, or that there is no alternative but to reorganize our way of life in order to survive the threat of terrorism. *The internalization of different versions of 'no alternative' stories has had the effect of contracting the space available for political life and calling into question the significance of the left–right divide.* As I argue in the next chapter, the acceptance of the culture of limits by left and right has led to this situation where politics is lost for words.

If indeed there is no alternative to the market or no alternative to reduced consumption then there is also no room for politics. The very idea of 'no alternative' implies both a lack of choice and the absence of the human capacity to make a difference. It represents a call for an end to political discussion and debate. In such circumstances, politics becomes an exercise in carrying out an administrative, technical or managerial function. That is why terms like 'bottom line', 'costed proposals', 'delivering services', 'scenario planning' or 'adding value' play such a prominent role in the contemporary political vocabulary. Policies are no longer characterized as good – they are 'evidence based'; they are rarely generated by a worldview, but are derived from 'best practice' and of course they are 'customer focused'. The colonization of public discourse by management-speak is the direct outcome not of the hidden hand of neo-liberal pressure but of the political exhaustion of society. As Watson argues, managerial language is a form of mechanized discourse that 'removes the need for thinking'.[14] That is why it has been so readily embraced by an unimaginative political class.

Political exhaustion

Politics seems to be running on empty. It has little in common with the passions and conflicts that have shaped people's commitments and sentiments over the past two centuries. There is no longer room for either the ardent defender of the free market faith, the proponent of traditional values or the robust advocate of the revolutionary transformation of society. The big issues of the past – the ownership and control of society's wealth, the production and allocation of resources, attitudes towards the future, science and experimentation – have been narrowed down to an occasional pleading for the homeless or the extremely frail pensioner. Heated debates tend to focus on issues that emanate from the imagination of an increasingly inwardly oriented political class. Public figures eschew big ideas and opt for a diet of micro-politics. Fox hunting, school dinners, abortion, licensing laws, university top-up fees, foundation hospitals are represented as the make-or-break questions of the twenty-first century. Political debates frequently erupt out of nowhere and catch politicians and commentators off-guard. At the same time, make-or-break issues suddenly vanish off the political radar. A few years ago Europe was represented as a crunch issue in British politics. During the 2005 General Election it simply disappeared from the public domain.

One symptom of political exhaustion is the disorientation of the ruling elites. They seem to lack a mission or a focus. Instead of attempting to inspire the electorate, governments appear to be in the business of counselling the populace towards lower expectations. As one of Britain's leading social theorists noted, 'unlike their ancestors of the nation-building era, global elites have no mission to perform; they do not feel the need or intend to proselytize, to carry the torch of wisdom, to enlighten, instruct and convert'.[15] With so little at stake, disagreements about policy issues frequently have the character of a squabble rather than of a debate. Public figures attempt to compensate for their petty posturing through adopting high-octane rhetoric. So, paradoxically, one of the consequences of decline of purpose and of genuine difference of substance is the escalation of the level of hatred and vitriol that different factions express towards one another. This trend was evident during the 2004 US Presidential campaign where, despite there appearing to be so little separating the candidates, many commentators remarked on the level of partisan rage and hostility.[16]

Partisan rage can often be misinterpreted as a symptom of deep ideological differences. The 'intensity of political polarization that grips the nation today is relatively new' wrote the Berkeley University academic Lillian Rubin.[17] Yet, as I argue in the next section, what appears as political polarization is actually a symptom of the absence of a clear alternative. What has happened is that people's identities and lifestyles have become politicized, as indicated by debates about same-sex marriage, religion, abortion, gun ownership and working parents. As one astute American commentator put it, the 2004 campaign 'strengthened the essential structure of the Two Americas, widened the gulf between the religious and secular, married and single, and gun owners and the unarmed'.[18] Differences in lifestyle do not necessarily lead to conflict. But when politicized, such issues have the capacity to generate emotion and tension. The fact that such private issues have become politicized indicates that the public sphere has become depoliticized.

Most serious social theorists are all too aware of the pervasive mood of political exhaustion. Back in 1997, Oxford political philosopher Isaiah Berlin remarked that 'for the first time since 1789 the European left does not have a project'. He could have

added that neither did the European right. This exhaustion of
politics is associated with widespread pessimism towards the
process of change. 'It is everywhere that ideas that were filled
with hope of liberation have lost their positive charge, have lost
all importance,' notes Alain Touraine, one of France's leading
sociologists.[19] Whilst there is widespread consensus about the
declining status of politics, there is a lack of clarity on how to
account for the emergence of this development.

The diminished status of politics is frequently associated with
a variety of economic, structural and technological changes
experienced in the last two or three decades. Many prominent
social scientists argue that the process of globalization has
undermined the traditions and institutions that underpinned
modern political life.[20] The spread of computers, the rise of the
Internet, the increase in service employment, the decline in
traditional manufacturing industries, the emergence of new
patterns of consumption, have all been offered as proof that we
live in a different political world.[21] Some argue that politics has
been overwhelmed by the sheer scale of economic and social
change.[22]

There is little doubt that in recent decades social and economic
life has undergone important changes. But why exciting
innovations like the Internet or increased global migration should
lead to a loss of the political imagination is far from clear. The
apparent suspension of political life is much more to do with the
loss of belief in the efficacy of human intervention than with the
power of insuperable economic or social forces. The very fact
that we point the finger at globalization as if it possesses divine
power to determine everything is itself symptomatic of a lack of
belief in society's capacity to manage change. The idea that
globalization sets in motion forces beyond human control
encourages the temptation to avoid responsibility for making
difficult choices and sticking with them.

The decline of politics is reflected in the different intellectual currents stimulated by the conservativism of fear rather than the triumph of neo-liberalism. In the 1980s the celebration of liberal free market principles could not be sustained in the face of economic stagnation. The ideas and arguments of Hayek and Friedman were rapidly overshadowed by the parallel emergence of two cultural responses: neo-conservatism and postmodernism. While welcoming the marginalization of radical critics of the market, neo-conservatives were preoccupied with what they perceived as the dangers of excessive individualism and the breakdown of community and tradition. This perspective regarded change – even that precipitated by Reagan and Thatcher – with ambiguity if not hostility. From this perspective, rebuilding, restoring and conserving the social fabric rent asunder by the ravages of market forces in the eighties became one of the principal tasks facing society.

The postmodernist sensibility is similarly deeply disenchanted with the consequences of change but recognizes that it is not possible to restore the traditions of the past. However, it also rejects any attempt to alter current circumstances, on the grounds that any such attempt is likely to make matters worse. In contrast to its neo-conservative cousin it has no positive ideals to promote. It expresses hostility to modernity and decries the 'Promethean' presumption of any 'human-centred' project. The very idea of politics is denounced as a myth, and the ideals of reason and progress are dismissed as a socially constructed fiction. This weary and nihilistic perspective counsels people to become reconciled to life as it is. It offers the most systematic expression of the sentiment of the conservatism of fear.

The conservatism of fear thrives through the promotion of a diminished sense of human potential. Those who celebrate the benefits of science and technology are frequently criticized for their 'irresponsible' lack of concern for the planetary ecosystem. The affirmation of the superiority of human reason over animal instinct risks being castigated as 'speciesism'. The denigration of humanity and the repudiation of the humanistic outlook that has been such a central feature of the development of modern civilization lurks behind the loss of contemporary political imagination. It provides the terrain on which the politics of fear can flourish.

This book argues that the main influence that shapes contemporary political life is the diminished role assigned to human agency. The culture of limits ascribes a very modest role to the subject, the active agency of human intervention. Those who decry the triumph of selfish egoism over solidarity today overlook the fact that the demise of old forms of solidarity – trade unions, local communities, mass political parties and political associations – has not led to the emergence of a dynamic individualism. One of the most commanding myths of our time is that contemporary culture celebrates and affirms a powerful sense of the individual. Nothing could be further from the truth. Though opinion makers and political leaders pay lip service to the importance of the individual, the 'rampant individualism' of the eighties is generally regarded with disdain. Indeed, the hedonistic and acquisitive values of the 1980s are blamed for many of the problems that we see today.

The restoration of politics does not depend on the discovery of clever ideas or new gimmicks designed to increase participation. It depends on restoring our confidence in the human potential through challenging the prevailing culture of limits. I hope that through a clearer understanding of the questions at stake it will be possible to outline a case for a future-oriented humanistic perspective. In order to do this, it is necessary to acknowledge that, in today's pre-political world, the fault line that divides us cannot be understood through the traditional categories of left and right. At least for now, the key question is where you stand in relation to the role human beings play in the making of their world. Is it the sense of human limitations or of human potential that shapes your view of the future and of the role of people in public life? How you view this question will determine whether you think politics matters and the choices we make have important consequences. No doubt at some time in the future there will be important arguments about the political values associated with the choices we make. But for now the differences that count are far more modest or arguably far more important. They are about whether or not we decide to realize our potential to choose and try to assume a measure of mastery over our circumstances. Understanding these basic issues will not change the world but it can help open a dialogue about how to respond to the forces that seek to estrange us from our humanity.

A case of American exceptionalism?

An American reader who has experienced the polarized atmosphere of the 2004 Presidential election may feel that politics is still alive and thriving in the United States. This sentiment is constantly echoed by the media, which frequently claims that the electorate is deeply divided and that society has become intensely polarized into Republican red and Democrat blue states. The vitriol that partisans of both sides direct towards one another may give the impression that politics is far from exhausted in the US. So how do we account for this apparent anomaly?

It is puzzling that such intense emotions were stimulated by an electoral contest where political and ideological differences were so slight between the two leading candidates. Both Bush and Kerry pledged to reduce the budget deficit by half. Kerry indicated that he would keep most of Bush's tax cuts, except those for the highest earners. Both promised to fight the war against terrorism with vigour. Despite appearances to the contrary, they were surprisingly close to one another on the question of same-sex marriage. A week before the election, Bush indicated that he disagreed with the Republican national

platform opposing same-sex civil union. Bush stated that he
opposed *Roe vs Wade*, the 1973 Supreme Court Ruling which
decriminalized abortion, but has repeatedly noted that America is
not ready to ban abortion. While Kerry did say he supported *Roe
vs. Wade*, he spoke in such convoluted terms about his support
for abortion rights that one was led to doubt his sincerity. He
constantly referenced his Catholicism to make clear that while he
personally opposed abortion he could not allow his religious
beliefs to get in the way of policy making. On questions such as
Medicare, health care, and social security, Kerry's message was
that 'the other guy's worse'.[23]

Paradoxically, despite the polarized rhetoric of the political
elites, the exhaustion of politics is even more developed in the US
than in most parts of the Western world. Public life has as its
premise the implicit assumption that politics is pointless. Why?
Because it is assumed that the vast majority of American voters
cannot be budged. It is claimed that there are two Americas – one
is red and the other is blue – and the election is decided by a tiny
percentage of swing voters. In the months leading up to the
election pundits frequently claimed that the electorate was so
polarized that only 2–3 per cent of the voters were undecided.[24]

If there are two Americas it is not politics that divides them.
The myth of a polarized America has been well documented.[25]
Significant sections of the electorate describe themselves as
moderate rather than as liberal or conservative, and more also
consider themselves as independents in preference to identifying
themselves as Democrats or Republicans.[26] Although many Bush
supporters were elated after the election, and Kerry supporters
correspondingly desolate, the underlying division is fuelled by the
adoption of different lifestyles.

Lifestyle and identity and not politics are what counts. Take
the view of one self-confessed liberal who is really worried about
'them'. She notes the difference between herself and her
'conservative friends' in the following way:

With one couple, it's a running joke: by mutual agreement, I do not urge abstract art, take them to experimental theatre, or suggest what they call 'eclectic' restaurants. They prefer the clarity of classical music; the abiding joys of Shakespeare; the reliability of steak, potatoes, and a vine of known vintage.[27]

Different attitudes to food and music also correspond to different characters. It is argued that 'half the people want righteous certainty at any cost – and a significant minority despises this certainty as ignorance, bigotry and cruelty'.[28] What is interesting about this counterposition of 'two moralities' is that it is all about attitudes and character traits. Quite rightly there is not a hint that crucial differences in political vision might be at stake.

Adolph Reed Jr from New School University cites the case of a colleague from an Ivy League campus who, after the 2004 election, complained that there are millions of people out there who are 'just not like us'. 'I realized that being a democrat for this colleague amounts to an existential statement, an announcement of the kind of person one is and that broadening a political base in an effort to win power or sharply change the terms of political debate was not at all her concern.'[29] Reed is right in pointing to the tendency to treat one's political identity as above all a matter of self-definition that gives expression to one's personality.

Of course once an individual's identity and political preference become entwined, arguments and debates can assume a highly charged personal form. Criticisms and arguments are perceived as if they represent a statement about the self and individual lifestyles. It was not political polarization but disputes about a way of life that led to the raising of the temperature during the 2004 election campaign.

To make matters worse, it is frequently suggested that the identity of those who inhabit the two camps is frozen and that they inhabit two very different realities. This was the argument of a report titled *The Separate Realities of Bush and Kerry*

Supporters by a group of University of Maryland academics. According to the report, Bush supporters live in a make-believe world whilst their opponents live in the real world.[30] Increasingly people's political attitudes are reduced to their character. Their family upbringing, their psychology and character, have become linked to political outcomes. An influential representative of this approach is George Lakoff. He divides the US electorate into two groups – those who adhere to a strict-father family and those adhering to a nurturant-parent family. Conservatives appeal to the outlook of the strict-father family. It is their 'strict authoritarian values' that 'motivate them to enter the voting booth'.[31] By contrast, progressives are imbued with the 'nurturant-parent worldview' and are inspired by the values of 'empathy and responsibility'.[32] Flattering the sensitive nurturing reader is incidental to Lakoff's project of associating people's voting behaviour as a personality issue rather than a matter of political choice.

The outlook conveyed through Lakoff's pop-psychology is that people's personality and identity are the immutable facts of life that determine how people vote. Authoritarian, strict-father types vote conservative and nurturing empathic ones will opt for the left. He rejects the idea that people vote in their self-interest. Otherwise how could they have re-elected Bush? Instead 'they vote their identity' and 'they vote their values'. In other words 'voters vote their identity – they vote on the basis of who they are, what values they have, and who and what they admire'.[33]

However, people's identity is far from fixed and certainly a simplistic association of parenting style with political affiliation overlooks the fluid and unpredictable manner in which people engage with public issues. And if identity has become an important factor that influences voting behaviour it has less to do with one's father figure than with the exhaustion of political life. At a time when, as we noted, there is very little to separate the candidates, politicians have sought to politicize people's lifestyles and personal life. Most of the wedge issues that divide the US electorate – guns, same-sex marriage, abortion, school prayer – directly impinge on people's identity. When issues become personal, debate becomes polarized. That is why in the US a sense of political stasis can coexist with heated debate.

Change and the possibility of influencing people's views is renounced once the idea of 'politics of choice' gives way to the 'politics of identity'. These sentiments are strikingly expressed through the widely held assumption that the political identity of 97 per cent of voters is fixed and unlikely to be changed through campaigning and debate. This trend is underpinned by the freezing of people's public identity. They are treated as if their lifestyles and values are as much part of their individuality as the colour of their skin or hair. The tendency to naturalize this identity is encouraged by the political elites, who appeal to it in order to consolidate a constituent.

One important study of this subject argues that what we have is a polarized elite rather than a polarized electorate. Morris Fiorina of Stanford University argues that it is 'political elites – pundits, activists, officeholders – who have a vested interest in dividing the country on issues like abortion and gay rights'.[34] But competition within the oligarchy should not be seen as a symptom of an active political culture. It is, as we suggest in the next chapter, a symptom of political disengagement.

2 Disengagement – and its Denial

Politics and politicians have an image problem. In today's anti-political times the way to succeed in electoral contests is by insisting that you are anything but a professional politician. Ronald Reagan showed that it helps if you are a well-known actor. Arnold Schwarzenegger's election as Governor of California indicated that you don't even have to be a particularly good actor to gain an important public office. Media mogul Silvio Berlusconi succeeded in becoming the President of Italy by playing the anti-politics card. So did former wrestling champion Jesse Ventura who got elected as Governor of Minnesota. In the UK, a far more modest but still significant achievement was the election of former TV personality Robert Kilroy-Silk as a member of the European Parliament, though, of course, he had previously been a Labour MP. The regular election of TV personalities and movie stars to national and local office in Asian countries like India and the Philippines indicates that the mood of anti-politics has become a global phenomenon.

The continuous disparagement of politicians in popular culture and the media suggests that what we are experiencing is not simply the exhaustion of politics but the rise of cynicism and even hostility to it. Some commentators, activists and protestors even celebrate the new mood of anti-politics as a healthy reaction against the corruption and cynicism of conventional politics. They interpret the declining popular influence of government, of parliament and the parliamentary parties, as proof that people have become less deferential and have adopted more critical attitudes. They welcome the loss of prestige of mainstream politics as an encouragement to the growth of the more informal new social movements and campaigns of the marginalized. So the author of a major study on the erosion of trust in politics claims that this trend can 'represent the driving force of democratic development'.[1] Another author celebrates the process of disengagement by rebranding it as a move *'away from deference'* and claims that people are now 'exerting more direct pressure through mechanisms outside the formal political process'.[2]

In fact, the affirmation of anti-politics expresses a profoundly pessimistic outlook towards the future. It represents a new form of deference. Whereas in the past people deferred to hierarchical authority, today they are encouraged to defer to Fate. Disengagement allows others to determine your fate. Anti-politics is not, as it sometimes appears, a rejection of particular parties and politicians, but an expression of a deeper conviction that politics as such is futile. The very idea that anybody could achieve any positive results through political action is often dismissed as naive or arrogant. But those who perceive some sort of radical imperative behind the rejection of politics ignore the fact that the flip-side of anti-politics is the acceptance of the world as it is. 'Politics is the denial of fate,' argues the Austrian political scientist Andreas Schedler.[3] Or to put it the other way around, anti-politics represents acquiescence to Fate.

Anti-politics is not so much an impulse towards empowerment as a gesture of resignation. Such an orientation implicitly calls into question the belief that people and their community can organize themselves purposefully to achieve some particular end. It is a perspective that belittles the potential of human action and the scope for progress. Anti-politics is simply an outlook that seeks to endow cynicism and mistrust with intellectual content.

The problem of political disengagement

Politicians have come to recognize that their political, ideological and moral links with the electorate are fragile. Traditional forms of party politics, political values and identities have little purchase on an evidently disenchanted public. Fewer and fewer people are prepared to vote, and fewer still are interested in getting involved in party politics. In the UK, membership of the major political parties has fallen by half since 1980. During the same period, political party membership in France has declined by two-thirds, and in Italy by 51 per cent. By comparison, the German figure looks good: total membership fell by only 9 per cent, probably because of an influx of new recruits from the east.[4]

The decline of party membership coincides with a wider disengagement from political life. Today, people's idealism and hopes are rarely invested in a belief in political change, and individuals rarely develop their identities through some form of political attachment. Thirty years ago, an individual might have identified herself as a Labour woman, whose outlook was shaped by her belief in a Socialist future and whose relationships in the present were with a community that shared this broad view. In the same way, for many members of the Conservative Party to be a Tory really meant something. It involved an important source of self-definition and involved participation in an active social network. Today the question of who you vote for is seen as barely significant, and self-identity is viewed far more in terms of individuals' lifestyles, cultural habits and personal experiences.

Popular mistrust of authority is confirmed by the growing alienation of people from the system of elections. American-style voting apathy has become a fact of life in the New Europe, where a significant proportion of the electorate believes that voting is a waste of time. The low turnout of voters affects the authority of governments who are keenly sensitive to the erosion of their legitimacy. Rather than renewing the political mandate, every

election threatens to become an embarrassing reminder of the
political wasteland that we inhabit. Apathy is no longer an
adequate term to describe the steady erosion of the public's
involvement in the political life of the United States. In almost
every presidential election since 1960, voter participation has
steadily declined – from 62.5 per cent of the electorate in 1960 to
50.1 per cent in 1988. During the election in 1996, only 49 per cent
of the voting-age population bothered to cast their ballots – the
lowest turnout since 1924. The election in 2000 continued this
pattern, with only about 50 per cent of registered voters
participating. The alienation of the public from the political
process was particularly striking in relation to the election of
2000. Unlike the election of 1996, where the outcome was seen to
be a foregone conclusion, the contest in 2000 was the most open
for decades. Yet the number of Americans who voted was
roughly the same as in 1996. According to the Committee for the
Study of the American Electorate, the cumulative effect of voter
disengagement during the past 30 years is that today, '25 million
Americans who used to vote no longer do so'. Yet voter
participation in presidential elections appears positively high
compared to the ballots cast for candidates running for a seat in
the House of Representatives. These averaged around 35 per cent
in the 1990s.

In the aftermath of 9/11, media pundits speculated that this
tragic event and the sense of patriotism to which it gave rise
might increase political participation. However, it soon became
evident that not even such a major event could disrupt the pre-
existing pattern of disengagement. The first 18 primaries prior to
5 July 2002 saw 'not just low turnout, but record low turnout –
with only eight per cent of Democrats and seven per cent of
Republicans going to the polls'.[5] At least during the November
2004 Presidential elections the steady decline in the turnout of
voters was halted. Voter turnout was 6.4 per cent higher than in
2000. However, it is worth noting that 78 million Americans who

were eligible to vote stayed at home and only 30.8 per cent of eligible voters cast their ballot for the winner, President Bush.[6]

European commentators should not feel smug about the passivity of the American electorate. In Britain, the facts speak for themselves. It is worth recalling that back in 1997, New Labour was backed by only 31 per cent of those qualified to vote. Voter turnout at this election was the lowest for 80 years. Even the much-hyped public relations campaign surrounding devolution in Scotland and Wales failed to engage the public's interest. Voter participation in these 'history-making' elections in 1999 indicated that the public regarded devolution as another stage-managed event. Only 46 per cent of the Welsh electorate voted, while in Scotland a high-profile media campaign designed to promote voter participation led to a turnout of 59 per cent, less than two-thirds. On the same day, polling booths in England were empty, with only 29 per cent of registered voters turning out for the 6 May local elections. The June 1999 UK elections to the European Parliament brought a turnout of 23 per cent – and in one Sunderland polling station, only 15 people turned up out of the 1000 entitled to vote. In the 2001 General Election, apathy emerged as the dominant issue under debate – and the turnout was an all-time low of 59 per cent. Tony Blair was returned to office with the backing of just 24 per cent of the electorate. He achieved the same feat in 2005 with the votes of only 22 per cent of those eligible to vote.

One of the most disturbing manifestations of the process of disengagement is that young people are even less inclined to vote than their elders. For example, during the 2001 General Election in Britain, the Electoral Commission estimated the turnout rate for 18–24-year-olds at only 39 per cent. As Weinstein notes 'as well as being less likely to vote in elections when compared with older age cohorts, young people have consistently fewer member-ships of formal groups of various kinds, express less interest in politics and are much less likely to offer a party political identification'.[7] An interesting study of electoral behaviour in Canada confirms the finding that the turnout of young people at elections is about 20 points lower than that of their elders. This generational dynamic is underpinned by attitudes that regard the act of voting as not a particularly important one.[8]

The steady decline of voter participation is directly linked to a much wider process. Lack of participation provides a clear index of disillusionment and public mistrust in the existing political system. Surveys of American public attitudes indicate that approval of the government has steadily declined in recent decades. Whereas in 1958, over 75 per cent of the American people trusted their government to do the right thing, only 28.2 per cent could express a similar sentiment in 1990. Since the beginning of this decade, trust in politicians has continued to decline. According to one study, between the mid-1960s and the mid-1990s the proportion of Americans who felt that 'the government is run by a few big interests looking out only for themselves' more than doubled to reach 76 per cent. In the same period the number who believed that 'public officials don't care about what people think' increased from 36 per cent to 66 per cent.[9]

A major study carried out by the Brookings Institution in May 2002 found that not even the wave of patriotism that followed in the aftermath of 9/11 translated into a durable growth of trust in the US Government. This survey showed that whereas in July 2001 only 29 per cent of Americans expressed a positive regard for their government, this figure almost doubled to 57 per cent in the aftermath of 11 September 2001. However, by May 2002, public trust in federal government had fallen back to 40 per cent, and experts felt that the opportunity for the reforging of a relationship of trust had already probably passed.[10]

Surveys in Europe point to a similar pattern. Studies carried out in the European Union indicate that around 45 per cent of the population is dissatisfied with the 'way that democracy works'. In

Britain, surveys reveal a high level of public cynicism towards politicians. A Gallup poll conducted in April 1995 concluded that most people's opinion of Members of Parliament was 'low' or 'very low'. A decade previously, only a third of people adopted this view. According to another survey, carried out in 1994, only 24 per cent of the population believed that the British Government places the national interest above party interests.[11] Politicians consistently come at the bottom of the list of professions that the public trusts. A survey published by the polling organization ICM in June 1999 found that only 10 per cent of the respondents stated that they trust politicians a lot, while 65 per cent trusted them a little, and 25 per cent not at all.[12] A study carried out by the BBC in February 2002 indicated that many people under the age of 45 regarded politicians as 'crooks', 'liars' and a 'waste of time'.[13]

During the 1990s, the erosion of public trust was reflected in a national mood of suspicion towards the political system itself. What emerged was a brand of anti-politics, a cynical dismissal of the elected politician and an obsession with sleaze and corruption in Westminster and Washington. The Clinton era was one of permanent scandal; and controversy surrounded the manner of Bush's election, only to be followed by a series of corporate scandals culminating in the Enron collapse. In 2005, allegations of financial misconduct against Tom DeLay, Republican leader in the House of Representatives, called into question the moral agenda he promoted as a voice of the so-called Religious Right.

New Labour's success at portraying the Conservatives as a party of sleaze was crucial to its electoral success of 1997 – but the New Labour Government quickly found that it was not immune to the politics of scandal. A spate of minor scandals involving Labour MPs and ministers followed the 1997 election victory, and the issue of sleaze continued to haunt the Government through 1998, as successive ministers were forced to resign. The suspicion that surrounds the manner in which Blair and Bush handled intelligence and information concerning weapons of mass destruction in Iraq is instructive in this respect. Instead of opposing the war in principle, critics of Blair and Bush prefer to look for scandals, and pontificate about conspiracies and cover-ups. Similar patterns are at work on the European continent. In Germany, charges of financial misdemeanour by the formerly governing Christian Democratic Union (CDU) surfaced soon after its defeat in 1998. This resulted in a scandal that rocked German politics for the best part of three years, from which conservative parties never recovered. In recent years scandal has become a regular feature of German political life, the most recent being the alleged illicit emoluments received by members of the German parliament.

In denial

Not everyone is concerned about the growing tendency towards disengagement and apathy. Traditional elite theories regard apathy as, on balance, a useful counterweight to the unpredictable consequences of the mobilization of mass movements. Back in the 1970s, the American political scientist Samuel Huntington warned that an 'excess of democracy' can be a problem for society. He believed that 'the effective operation of a democratic political system usually requires some measure of apathy and non-involvement on the part of some individuals and groups'.[14] This celebration of disengagement has been traditionally associated with the anti-democratic ethos promoted by sections of the right-wing intelligentsia. Today, however, such a cavalier attitude towards the consequences of disengagement is no longer confined to right-wing commentators who are suspicious of popular participation in the electoral process. Researchers and commentators often minimize the scale of the problem of apathy.

They frequently peddle the myth that there is in fact no real problem of disengagement.

The tendency to deny the reality of political exhaustion is expressed through a variety of arguments. Some accept that political apathy and disengagement is widespread but insist that its dimension is exaggerated. Others argue that the problem only afflicts traditional party and electoral politics. They point to the involvement of people in protests, non-governmental organizations (NGOS) and self-help groups as evidence that people are no less actively involved in political life than previously. Such complacent attitudes are often justified on the Panglossian grounds that politics has changed – and probably for the better. According to one account 'the repertoire of political action ... has broadened since the 1960s and 1970s to include a range of direct or uninstitutionalized forms of action – petitions, demonstrations, citizen initiatives, political strikes'.[15]

This claim that the meaning of politics has changed requires an ever-expanding definition of political activism. People filling in online petitions or ticking a few boxes on one of 1.5 million sites on the web are treated as the equivalent of the active citizen. It appears that virtually every form of activity and public gesture is associated with the term politics. That is why we now routinely speak of the politics of the body, the politics of food, the politics of health, the politics of cancer, the politics of victimization, and the politics of language, or of the personal as political. By endowing a bewildering variety of activities with the status of political, it is possible to claim that ours is a lively political culture. Through expanding the definition of politics, the prevailing process of depoliticization can be reinterpreted as the creative widening of the sphere of activism and participation. From this perspective, it is even possible to contend that a 'common theme in almost all advanced industrial democracies is the expansion of the political agenda over the past several decades, and the emergence of new political actors to represent new issues'.[16] The process defined as the expansion of the political agenda can be better understood as a rapid growth of *micro-politics*.

One strategy for inflating the meaning of politics is to apply it to describe routine and everyday activities. Anthony Giddens' concept of 'life politics' does precisely that. As one of the principal intellectual architects of the Third Way, Giddens is self-consciously upbeat about what he calls the advent of 'life politics'. He believes that today's social movements and self-help groups possess important democratic qualities and therefore represent an advance over the traditional style of party politics. 'In contemporary societies, far more people belong to self-help groups than are members of political parties,' he observes.[17] The implication of this statement is that not only is the act of participating in a patients' self-help group comparable to membership of a political party but it also represents a positive advance over it. Obviously if every form of engagement is redefined as political it is possible to offer a very optimistic view of the current situation. Writing in this vein, Giddens presents a glowing account of civic engagement:

> There are signs that interest in politics is actually on the rise, but is simply being channelled into directions other than orthodox party politics. Membership in civic groups and associations is growing and activists are devoting their energies to new social movements focused around single issues such as the environment, trade policy and nuclear non-proliferation.[18]

The idea that 'interest in politics is actually on the rise' can only possess a semblance of plausibility if it is equated with involvement in a parenting class, a therapy circle or a local campaign for traffic speed restrictions. Expanding the definition of political activity provides the foundation for the illusion that public life is thriving.

Those who are worried about the disconnection of the twenty-first-century public from political life are frequently dismissed with the argument that their concerns are based on a very 'old-fashioned' perception of participation. One influential exponent of this conformist attitude is the political scientist Pippa Norris. She asserts that concern with the present state of political disengagement is driven by a nostalgia for the past. Norris warns of 'the danger of mythologizing a romantic Golden Age when all the town hall meetings were packed, all the voting booths were overflowing, and all the citizens were above average'. She adds that 'familiar patterns of our parents' and grandparents' generations are regarded nostalgically as the norm, in a misty-eyed Jimmy Stewart small-town-America sort of way'.[19] Her dismissive attitude towards the past is matched by an uncritical embrace of the present. Indeed, this disparagement of old-fashioned attitudes towards participation is motivated by a profound conformist sensibility. The politics of the past is criticized in order to affirm the so-called activism of today.

Norris sees political activism wherever she looks. She states that 'new social movements, transnational policy networks and Internet activism offer alternative avenues of engagement'.[20] She believes that if anything the public is more active then before since 'demonstrations, signing petitions, and consumer boycotts have become far more common since the mid-1970s'.[21] She adds that protest movements have 'moved from margin to mainstream' and that the public is genuinely engaged in them. Later in this chapter we shall have an opportunity to evaluate the meaning of contemporary movements of protest. But for now it is worth noting that many of the forms of protest held up as evidence of a new era of activism – the signing of petitions, consumerist activities – can be interpreted as a retreat towards a privatized and passive form of public behaviour. These are forms of protests that have the character of a public gesture and make no pretence of offering an alternative.

Passive and atomized forms of public involvement reflect the temper of our time. More people write to local councillors, MPs and newspapers, and complaints to the ombudsman between 1976 and 1992 have doubled in relation to health and increased by a factor of 10 in local government matters. The workloads of bodies such as Citizens Advice Bureaux, law centres, the Equal Opportunities Commission and the Commission for Racial Equality have increased massively over the past two decades. In the US, litigation and demand for compensation continues to increase, whilst in the UK there has been a dramatic explosion in such claims.[22] It would appear that these semi-official bodies have taken up the strain of dissatisfaction expressed in an individualized form, as the scope for collective protests has narrowed.

The new politics of protest does not represent any advance over conventional forms of representative democracy. Unlike the genuine protest movements from the past, today's highly institutionalized activism provides little scope for participation. 'The great majority of the 5 million people who are officially members of one of the organizations that make up the environmental movement, for example, are fairly passive, rarely extending beyond possession of their membership card,' notes one observer.[23] It is easy to overlook the fact that high-profile public protest frequently involves small numbers of professional activists. What counts is not the mobilization of grass-roots support but an effective media strategy. Theda Skocpol's study of American non-profit groups provides compelling evidence that these are organizations run by a professional oligarchy. 'Professionally managed, top-down civic endeavours simultaneously limit the mobilization of most citizens into public life', she observes.[24]

Another way in which the significance of disengagement is minimized is by suggesting that it represents not apathy but an understandable reaction to an unresponsive government. One commentary on the situation in France states that 'the spontaneous street protests confirm that voters are not apathetic about democracy, rather they are dissatisfied with the current model of government and the unresponsive nature of government'.[25] This argument is frequently used to minimize the troublesome phenomenon of youth apathy.

Empirical research consistently provides evidence of the disconnection of young people from political life. Nevertheless, some commentators attempt to avoid confronting this problem by attempting to define it out of existence. They contrive to delude themselves that young people are 'engaging in alternative ways'.[26] It is said that the declining participation of young electors 'should not be taken as evidence of youth apathy or indifference to all things political' since it may only be a 'problem for a particular *kind* of politics'.[27] Indeed the argument is sometimes formulated in a way that suggests that whatever young people do must be political – whether they know it or not. 'Young people are more likely to participate in voluntary groups rather than in political parties' but 'they do not necessarily regard this participation as "political" in itself', argues an introduction to a discussion on this subject.[28]

The literature on youth disengagement often redefines the issue as the problem of the alienation of young people. It argues that young people are interested in social issues and want to get involved but since nobody listens to them they become demoralized and disengaged. One British study devoted to questioning the thesis of 'youth apathy' states that young people are 'highly articulate about the political issues that affect their lives, as well as about the disconnection between these and mainstream politics'. It adds that 'they don't feel that anyone in authority, and especially in central government, is listening to them'.[29] A closer inspection of this argument indicates that all this has little to do with real politics. There is little doubt that young people can be 'highly articulate' about issues that affect them. But all this means is that they can engage intelligently with the everyday issues they confront. Normally this characteristic is associated with the act of getting on with life. Flattering the youth for being interested in those aspects of life that directly affect them says more about the prevailing attitude of low expectations than about a renewed orientation towards politics.

Another way that the problem of youth disengagement is minimized is to claim that the problem lies with the way that political life is experienced by young people. Political institutions that are aloof and unresponsive, politicians who do not listen to the public, and a sense of estrangement from decision making are often presented as factors that account for youth disengagement.[30] There is little doubt that the institutions of political life suffer from many defects. Many governments and politicians are inflexible and unresponsive to the needs of ordinary people. However, governments and political institutions have always suffered from a democratic deficit and other defects. That is why the quality of decision making and distribution of power cannot account for youth disengagement today. If young people want to become active they will do so regardless of the way their political institutions operate. Feeling excluded and marginalized has never stopped young people from getting stuck in. Nor do young people necessarily withdraw from public life if politicians do not listen to them. In 1917 in Czarist Russia, the average age of leading Bolsheviks was 26 and most party members were in their teens. Young students led the protests in Tiananmen Square in Beijing in 1989 precisely to force politicians to listen to them.

The problem today is not the failure of politicians to listen to the electorate. Even if they listened harder not much would change. Disengagement is underwritten by a powerful sense of political exhaustion. And the impulse to deny the reality of disengagement and celebrate the new forms of activism and protest is a testimony to the influence of complacency and conformism in the contemporary imagination. Often the response of cynicism is confused with criticism and the tendency towards disconnecting with the political process is sometimes celebrated as a responsible act of a critical citizen. It is even claimed that recent decades have seen the emergence of a 'new type of critical citizen' who is dissatisfied with the democratic process but who nevertheless remains strongly committed to democratic values.[31] A strong version of this argument is advanced by Giddens, who sees in the activities of self-help groups and single-issue campaigns a launching pad for the expansion of greater democracy.

It is difficult when confronted with the fact that people are less and less interested in politics, to sustain the argument that we live in a world where a critical citizenry stands ready to democratize democracy. The statement 'politics is boring' does not simply refer to a response to a particular event or politician. It represents an outlook that regards politics as an irrelevant pastime. That is why a growing section of the population takes little interest in the subject and spends less time reading or watching the news. Young people in particular show little interest in public affairs because they do not consider caring about such things to be important. An interesting Canadian study found that the younger generations vote less frequently then their elders because 'they tend to attach less importance or value' to voting than others.[32] According to the authors this attitude is the product of important cultural influences that work to diminish the status of politics.

Disengaged protest

The mood of disengagement has even succeeded in engulfing movements of protest. Protest has become a strikingly personal matter. It is frequently about the protester as an individual, and says more about how people feel about themselves than about what they think about the issue at stake. That is why it is often difficult to define today's acts of protest as constituting a political movement. On the contrary, they are the product of the prevailing mood of isolation and disengagement.

Yet one frequently hears the argument that the public's disenchantment with the political order provides an opportunity for the flourishing of radical dissent. Norris believes that recent 'anti-capitalist demonstrations' 'have rocked summits of world leaders from Seattle to Quebec, Gothenberg and Genoa, forcing reconsideration of issues of debt repayment by poorer nations'.[33] Similar claims were also made about the impact and effectiveness of protest marches against the military invasion of Iraq in 2003. Many veterans of leftist protest were delighted when a million or so people in the UK turned out in February 2003 to march against the war. Claims that these were the biggest anti-war protests since Vietnam, not to mention the first protest in over a decade to attract a sizable number of young people, expressed the hope that the reaction against the Iraq war was spawning the kind of radical political movement last seen in the 1970s. Radical commentators have not addressed the fact that these one-off mass events have not spawned a legacy of grass-roots protest. And very little has been said about how quickly these ineffectual flash-in-the pan media events vanished from the public domain.

The pendulum swings like this because commentators mistake confusion and distrust of the political system or suspicion towards authority for an inherently progressive response. They are then quickly confronted by the cynicism, passivity and a sense of fatalism that such distrust resolves itself into under circumstances where 'There Is No Alternative'. Acceptance of TINA does not preclude acts of protest – but it means that such protests express the politics of disengagement. It was fitting that one of the most prominent slogans of the movement against the 2003 invasion of Iraq was 'Not In My Name'; a self-consciously personal proclamation. It is not a political statement designed to involve others, and does not seek to offer an alternative. It does not call on anyone to choose sides or even insist on a particular course of action. 'Not in my name' says 'don't involve me'. It is not so much a position towards an issue as a declaration that

insists 'I don't want anything to do with this at all.' Like its
parent slogan 'Not In My Backyard', the slogan expresses the
narrow orientation of disconnected protest. It represents an opt-
out clause, rather than an attempt to alter the course of events; a
shrug of the shoulder, which reflects a mood of general anti-
engagement as much as it does a weariness towards war.

That is why, despite the mobilization of millions on the streets
of Western capitals, these protests have had such little impact on
society. Despite the fact that so many opposed the war, the
absence of passion or belief in the protest making a difference
meant that the large numbers never amounted to a movement, at
least in the old sense of the term. The personal presentation of
anti-war sentiment contains an implicit renunciation of social
activism and political protest.

Of course disengagement is a contested concept. Certainly,
people out on the streets of London or Seattle, protesting 'against
capitalism' or the invasion of Iraq, do not think of themselves as
disengaged. Today's activists continually point out the large size
of many recent demonstrations. However, understanding the
dynamic of mobilizations and protest cannot be gained through
just counting numbers. Since the end of the Cold War in the early
1990s, we have seen on numerous occasions the phenomenon of
self-consciously apolitical public mobilizations. The public outburst of emotionalism around the death of Princess Diana; the so-
called White Movement in Belgium, sparked by the appalling
Dutroux child murders of the late 1990s; the US Evangelical
Men's Movement 'The Promise Keepers'; and the UK vigilante
protests against paedophiles have been driven by groups of people
who are committed to making their own personal statement.

There are many activists who feel that their individual acts
represent a valid form of engagement. No doubt they do. But for
engagement to have a social and political dimension it needs to be
directed towards influencing the wider public. It is not simply a
personal statement but also part of a wider communal project.

Engagement expresses an orientation towards interaction with others. It is undertaken as part of a wider public dialogue that seeks to establish or alter the prevailing consensus on an issue or issues.

The clearest expression of the absence of such an orientation can be seen in what is often depicted as the most attractive feature of contemporary social movements: their sheer numbers and diversity. The World Social Forum, like other protest movements, frequently boasts that what distinguishes it from others is its diversity. However, this celebration of diversity may be a strategy for making a virtue out of the fact that this Forum is a diffuse, fragmented and atomized collection of pressure groups. According to one account 'what is most surprising, and more important, is how despite ... differences, the movement retains some coherence and unity'.[34] But it is a unity based on an unquestioning and uncritical endorsement of the idea of not questioning one another. Unlike true tolerance – which implies tolerating what we dislike – diversity is an apolitical strategy for avoiding making statements of judgement.

The great variety of organizations that are called movements is truly breathtaking. It is claimed that the large variety of social movements is necessitated by the plurality of experiences and meanings in contemporary society.[35] However, it can also be argued that the pluralization of experience is not so much a natural fact of life, but a self-conscious rejection of engaged dialogue. The attitude of 'live and let live' can be seen either as a form of enlightened tolerance or as the renunciation of engagement through dialogue. I fear that it may represent the latter.

In the past the self-conscious cultivation of sectional interests was frequently characterized as sectarian. These days we don't use the word sectarian too often because movements are generally not inclined (or can't be bothered) to wrangle with one another. Yet such attitudes bear an uncanny resemblance to old-fashioned sect-like attitudes, in particular in their lack of interest in influencing the wider public. They are bound up with the orientation of contemporary movements to issues associated with identity and lifestyle. One of the most significant manifestations of political disengagement is the reconfiguration of activism as a form of lifestyle choice. Murray Bookchin's critique of 'lifestyle anarchism' provides an astute analysis of the way that the motif of self-expression comes to define the parameters of a particular form of activism.[36] A similar critique could be made of a variety of other lifestyle-, identity- or consumer-focused organizations.

The politics of self-expression are extremely influential because they are continually affirmed through the media and popular culture. Indeed, self-expression is validated as a genuine and authentic act and is often favourably contrasted to what is perceived as the estranged artificial world of politics. The Italian sociologist Alberto Melucci claims that one of the distinct features of contemporary social movements is that people's participation within movements is no longer a means to an end but an end in itself. 'Participation in collective action is seen to have no value for the individual unless it provides a direct response to personal needs.'[37] A proponent of 'direct action' is besotted with the 'personal power that being one of so many people moving in the same direction can give you'.[38] The idea of regarding participation as providing therapeutic benefits is argued for in the following terms: 'Strong feelings for the group make participation pleasurable in itself, independently of the movement's ultimate goal and outcomes.'[39]

When protest is embraced because of its alleged therapeutic benefits, the link between protest and the politics of change becomes ruptured. There is nothing objectionable about individuals participating in organizations in order to become members of an emotional community. However, when the pursuit of self-discovery becomes a principal objective of involvement it is likely to turn into merely another form of disengagement.

During the past decade some of the largest mobilizations in Europe have been influenced by this trend of expressing 'personal needs'. The occasions often assume the character of a personal quest for meaning – a form of individual pilgrimage. In July 1997 there was a mass demonstration in Spain to mourn the murder of Miguel Angel Blanco by Basque separatists. The event unleashed a strange emotional dynamic. At times the crowd exuded a sense of intensity as if something tragic was just about to happen. At other times, a sense of anticipation – not unlike at pop festivals – helped create a feeling of exhilaration. Demonstrators told interviewers that they were not sure why they were there and some suggested that they too felt like victims. This reaction was self-consciously cultivated by the crowd with the gesture of placing their hands at the back of their heads in the posture of surrendering prisoners. A similar response was evident amongst the crowd that congregated in Rome during the funeral of Pope John-Paul II.

Regrettably, the crowds that thronged the streets of Rome, like the protestors that wished to vent their anger against George W. Bush, are no more engaged with society than are the people who watch their activities at home on TV. They, too, are mainly in the business of making a personal statement. Above all, they are motivated to take to the streets by the impulse to find meaning, and do not think very much about how to influence others. It is a lonely crowd indeed.

Conclusion

It is difficult to quantify the process of disengagement. Mental and cultural attitudes towards one's community and institutions are difficult to translate into the language of figures. Practices like voting or participating in meetings acquire different meanings in different circumstances. In recent times the postal ballot has been extended by the UK Government in order to make it easier for people to vote. But does mailing a postal ballot, written out in response to pressure from a party activist visiting a pensioner at home, have the same meaning as the public act of voting?

Nor is political apathy a problem exclusive to our time. For example, during the 1950s considerable anxieties were expressed about the so-called 'silent generation' of apathetic youth in the United States. It was claimed that young people had switched off from politics because they had become preoccupied with their economic security and private life.

However, any resemblance between the silent generation of the 1950s and voter apathy today is a superficial one. The mood of cynicism that prevailed in the 1950s was confined to a relatively narrow stratum of educated middle-class youths and intellectuals. The rest of society remained relatively engaged. Unlike today, the politics of anti-politics were relatively insignificant and individuals tended to take their political affiliations seriously. In the 1950s politics still mattered. Despite the emergence of a consensus around the desirability of a mixed economy, the public was regularly confronted with a clash of alternatives. The distinction between left and right still meant something very important to people. Politics may have stagnated and often it was not very exciting but it had not yet become exhausted. What possible meaning left and right can have today is the subject of the next chapter.

3 Left and Right – How the Words Lost their Meaning

The most striking manifestation of the process of political exhaustion has been the erosion of the meaning of the terms *left* and *right*. Since the years leading up to the French Revolution, left and right stood for radically different ways of engaging with society. The first important controversy in the French revolutionary National Assembly testified to the importance of the distinction between left and right. In this debate the right advocated the separation of political power whilst the radical left supported the ideal of full popular sovereignty. Since the eighteenth century, conflict between left and right over the role of the state and of government, the management of economic life, attitudes towards capitalism, the significance attached to democracy, the meaning of rights, the status of the individual, the role of religion in society and of science have dominated political life. This conflict was not confined to the domain of politics. It involved a different orientation towards such basic questions as the meaning of human nature – whether it is determined by nurture (left) or nature (right) and the role of tradition and morality. Nor was this a conflict confined to small groups of politicians and intellectuals. During the past two centuries millions of people have been mobilized by political parties wedded to distinct ideologies. And the conflict between parties of the left and right has provoked revolutions, counter-revolutions, upheaval and violence. The conflict between left and right also possessed a creative dimension. Throughout most of modernity, both sides were forced to account for themselves, rethink their ideals and develop new insights about the nature of society. Their disagreement has also produced a rich philosophical and political tradition of debate.

There is little that remains of the political left and right in the twenty-first century. There are of course many individuals who still think of themselves as left-wing or right-wing. Commentators frequently talk about the 'Labour Left', and New Labour frequently denounces the 'right-wing Tories'. In the US, the Democrats, or at least a section of them, are described as left while the Republicans are depicted as right wing. However, a closer inspection of public life suggests that these terms have lost much of their historic relevance. Left and right have become words in search of meaning. People who define themselves according to old ideological labels do so as individuals and as a matter of self-definition. And they do so in isolation from a wider movement because of the absence of a living left- or right-wing political tradition. What we have are individuals, but not projects or movements that are associated with the classical meaning of left or right. As we noted in the previous chapter, even protest campaigns avoid any explicit association with a political project.

The various protest movements currently campaigning against globalization and capitalism express the depoliticized mood of our time. These movements self-consciously eschew 'ideology' and political projects. Their supporters continually boast that they stand for 'tolerance of plurality, diversity and openness'.[1] Some speak in terms of a 'space' rather than a 'movement' and insist that 'no-body in the [Social] Forum has the power or the right to say that one action or proposal is more important than another'.[2] They explicitly distance themselves from 'big ideas' and ideology and are even reluctant to debate political differences. According to one account this movement 'is so frightened of shattering its often fragile unity, or developing a hierarchy that would enable the more powerful and influential activists to push all the others around, that there is an almost pathological fear of airing differences in public and potentially "splitting the movement" '.[3] This reaction to debate is so intense that the movement has internalized a powerful strand of anti-politics. It is a movement that defines itself not by what it stands for but by its form of organization. According to one of its supporters, 'new forms of organisation *are* its ideology'.[4] In Germany the Greens make much of their contribution to the cleansing of society of ideology. Antje Vollmer, deputy chairperson of the Bundestag and founding member of the Green movement, believes that as a result, 'The European world is no longer frightened of the Germans because we have civilised this country thoroughly.'[5]

The demise of Socialism has been widely commented on. However it is important to realize that other political ideals have also suffered a similar fate. According to Giddens, 'conservative thought has become largely dissolved'. Some adherents of conservatism agree with this pessimistic diagnosis of events. The British commentator John Gray has argued that the 'conditions under which conservatism as a coherent form of political thought and practice are possible exist no longer'.[6]

The growing irrelevance of the terms left and right is often attributed to a tendency on the part of politicians and parties to occupy the centre. Sometimes this process is seen as the result of the convergence of left and right parties. There are numerous precedents whereby political parties have sought to gain electoral advantage by occupying the centre. This tactic was frequently deployed by both the Labour and Conservative Parties in post-war Britain. However, this pursuit of the politics of the centre is different to the dynamic at play today. Centrist governments today are not simply involved in maintaining a balancing act between left and right. They are in the business of distancing themselves from any distinct political associations. They are not so much centrist as avowedly apolitical. This orientation is systematically pursued by organizations identified with the Third Way. 'New Labour's Third Way project does not involve simply taking up a position at another point on the spatially configured left–right scale,' argues an insightful study on the subject. Rather, it adds, 'it is about largely rejecting the very idea of a political scene organized on an adversarial – left versus right – basis'.[7] The Third Way is not the cause but the beneficiary of the legacy of the decline of left and right.

The process of party convergence in the interwar years and the Cold War is different to contemporary times. Previous attempts to occupy the centre ground by stealing the clothes of one's opponents did not necessarily lead to the suspension of political conflict. In the 1940s and 50s the shift of the right to the centre merely altered the way that political conflict was played out. But in the 1980s the transformation of parties of the left into centrist ones has had a more far-reaching consequence because it coincided with a powerful mood of political exhaustion. Increasingly, the decisions and policies adopted by governments appear as pragmatic ones that bear little relationship to politics. Politicians are not so much in the business of convincing as selling their policies. As Richard Reeves observed, 'ideology is a dirty word in New Labour circles' but 'without ideology, the role of politicians is no longer to persuade, merely to sell'.[8] In the US and the UK selling a political brand involves spending millions on advertising. In the US, it even means paying newspaper columnists to promote your policies.[9]

Why the words lost their meaning

A variety of structural changes – globalization, the growing fluidity of economic and social existence, the weakening of class and national identities, the trend towards individuation, the orientation towards consumption and lifestyle, the emergence of new uncertainties in a complex world – are seen as responsible for both the exhaustion of politics and the decline of left and right. In an influential contribution to this discussion, Giddens argues that 'if the terms right and left no longer have the meaning they once did, and each political perspective is in its own way exhausted, it is because our relationship (as individuals and as humanity as a whole) to modern social development has shifted'. He claims that since 'we live today in a world of manufactured uncertainty' and 'high consequence risks', we can only grapple with the future and therefore the more ambitious politics of vision is doomed.[10] Other contributions point to the ascendancy of information technology, the Internet, the increase in service employment, the decline in traditional manufacturing industries, and the emergence of new patterns of consumption, as factors that may be responsible for the decline of politics.

Other commentators often associate the process of globalization and the declining influence of national governments with the decline of politics and of political ideologies. For example, Bauman claims that the association of politics with a distinct geographic territory is 'fast losing its importance'. 'No wonder that "grounded politics" of past ages rapidly runs out of substance,' he argues.[11] There is little doubt that the changing character of social and economic structures has had a significant impact on the way that people make choices and experience their public life. However, it is unlikely that changes to the structure and economic organization of society are the direct cause of the exhaustion of politics. It is worth noting that change, uncertainty and disruption have been the norm during the past three centuries. The industrial revolution served as a catalyst for the sudden rise of urban centres and global migration in the nineteenth century. Insecurity associated with upheavals in the world economy, two World Wars, the threat of a nuclear one, and the Cold War indicates that uncertainty is the norm in the modern world. Today's tendency to see politics as the victim of economic and social change tends to objectify what is more likely a loss of political imagination. In particular, the elevation of the process of globalization into a force beyond human intervention is itself a reflection of the mood of fatalism that is a product of political exhaustion. The objectification of the causes of political decline is not simply a statement about the present situation but an argument that forecloses the possibility of the revival of serious alternatives in the future.

Representatives of both the left and the right have sought to account for the diminishing plausibility of their ideals by finding refuge in economic or structural explanations. Both sides of the old political divide are happy to blame the decline of both class and community solidarity on the liberalization of the world market. Leftist thinkers in particular have often blamed the demise of the left on changes in the way that society works and the lives which people lead. Such arguments often represent a roundabout way of echoing the mantra that there is no alternative. And indeed the claim that the distinction between left and right has lost its salience is linked to the proposition that politics has come to an end because reality dictates that there is no alternative.

It seems important to distinguish the fate of the left and right from the question of whether or not politics has come to an end. Today it is far from clear what is left and what is right. Certainly, when it comes to the formal political process the terms have very little meaning. And, as we shall show, even when it comes to the politics of protest the distinction between left and right is far from evident. However, the fact that this distinction has little salience today does not mean that there cannot be important differences between political movements in the future. The erosion of the distinction between left and right today should not inevitably lead to the conclusion that important political differences and conflict will never return.

What the explanations outlined above all have in common is the tendency to objectify the process whereby the categories left and right have become irrelevant. This endows the exhaustion of political life with an aura of inevitability. Yet such an interpretation tends to be based on the sloppy habit of reading history backwards. From this perspective the outcome of history is naturalized and turned into an inescapable consequence of past developments. But it is neither the process of globalization nor the rise of new technology that has precipitated the exhaustion of political life and the decline of the left and right. In principle, people and society can respond to social change in a variety of different ways. Today's political impasse is only one possible outcome amongst many other possibilities. The decline of left and right is the outcome of historical experiences that have served to undermine the credibility of competing movements. It is possible to isolate three important historical moments that have served a crucial role in undermining the credibility of both the left and the right: these were the Second World War, the Cold War and the Culture Wars of the eighties.

The Second World War forced the right on to the defensive, particularly on the intellectual front. The association of right-wing ideas with fascism and the perceived causes of war forced explicitly conservative ideas to the margins of social thought. As Daniel Bell, a leading American sociologist, remarked, since the Second World War, right-wing ideologies 'were inevitably discredited' and in Europe 'no single right-wing figure retained any political credibility or influence'.[12] There were attempts to distance the right from any association with the Nazi experience. Karl Popper in his *Open Society and its Enemies* blamed the spiritual breakdown occasioned by Marxism for the growth of fascism. And Hayek in his influential text *The Road to Serfdom* sought to depict Nazism as the logical extension of Socialism. However, these attempts to limit damage could do little more than minimize the scale of the setback suffered. As Paul Piccone, the maverick American social theorist, points out, the 'World War II defeat of fascism and Nazism led to the criminalization not only of both of these ideologies but of the "Right" in general'.[13]

The right's setback allowed – albeit temporarily – even the Soviet Union to gain a degree of credibility. This was a period when both conservative and liberal thinkers were on the defensive. Even in the period of the long post-war economic boom, many supporters of the West lacked the confidence to mount a full-blooded defence of the free market against alternative models. Symptomatic of this lack of belief in the virtues of capitalism was the approach adopted by the French sociologist Raymond Aron. He argued that 'doctrinal disputes' were a 'thing of the past' and that all 'regimes are imperfect' and neither the US nor the Soviet Union was all that bad.[14] By emphasizing the similarities of the two systems, Aron, like other theorists of convergence, gave up the attempt to construct a positive vision based on the unique tradition of Western capitalism. Instead of stating that 'we are morally superior', convergence theory suggested that 'you are no better than us'.

During the Cold War, intellectual supporters of capitalism sought to consolidate their position through defining themselves against Communism. The West was able to strengthen its credibility through contrasting its way of life with the economic deficiencies and the oppressive character of the Soviet regimes. However, the right was not able to construct a positive worldview based on the celebration of the virtues of capitalist society. By the 1960s it was clear that the real problem for the upholders of the Western capitalist tradition was not the dynamism of its ideological opponents but its own deficiencies. The only positive claim that they could confidently propose was that the capitalist system worked better than slowly disintegrating societies of the Stalinist world. But the advocates of the claim of economic efficiency could not develop an idea of a greater purpose that could inspire the public.

The left, too, came unstuck during the Cold War. In the end, conservative and liberal political currents thrived because more and more people became repelled by virtually every aspect of the Soviet-type society. The Cold War did not do much to revitalize the right but it did much to undermine the left. By the seventies many of the initiatives associated with the left – planned economies, the Welfare State – stood exposed and discredited. And, indeed, by the late 1970s it was the ideas of the left that appeared exhausted and irrelevant. The apparent failures of Stalinism in Eastern Europe, of radical Third World regimes and of the social-democratic welfare state in the West dealt a severe blow to the ideas traditionally associated with these developments. In a sense the failure of these alternatives allowed the right to turn the tables on their opponents and win the Cold War.

At the end of the 1980s it appeared for a brief moment that the end of the Cold War had helped to revitalize conservatism and the politics of the right. But only for a moment. Instead of boosting confidence, the West's triumph in the Cold War merely revealed an absence of purpose and vision. The quest among leading Western politicians for a 'big idea' to replace the anti-Communist crusade of the post-war decades has failed to discover one. As one contributor to a post-Cold War discussion of the 'Winds of Change' put it, a 'plausible vision of the common good remains stubbornly elusive'.[15] Observers rightly noted the political exhaustion of the alternatives to Western liberalism but what they failed to notice was the demise of the so-called Western idea as well. It was during the Culture Wars of the late twentieth century that the exhaustion of the right became evident. This process was temporarily obscured by the success of neo-liberal political parties in the eighties. The Thatcher-Reagan years were associated with the triumph of right-wing ideology. However, the emergence of a neo-liberal consensus in the economic sphere was not matched by a similar process in the political. Indeed, in the sphere of culture, traditional conservative ideals regarding tradition, the family, sexuality and morality were on the defensive. Paradoxically, this triumphalist neo-liberal moment coincided with the institutionalization of many of the values associated with the cultural left. What came to be celebrated was not the 'Western idea' but more relativistic virtues such as diversity, multiculturalism and difference. As Adam Meyerson complained in 'A Conservative Research Agenda for the 90s' – a contribution to the American publication *Policy Review*, of which he was the editor – 'as communism collapses, the greatest ideological threat to western civilization now comes from within the West's own cultural institutions – universities, the churches, the professions such as law and medicine, and above all the disintegrating family'.[16]

The Culture Wars revealed that neither side in the political divide could recover from its state of intellectual exhaustion. They indicated that the right could discredit the left but not generate a positive account of itself that could provide a viable alternative. In turn the cultural left was able systematically to discredit many of the traditions and values associated with the right. But it did so not through developing a positive view of the world but through echoing and amplifying the prevailing mood of apathy and cynicism. In particular, it fed off the prevailing sense of confusion and promoted the claim that no ideals could possess universal relevance and that claims to Truth should be held in suspicion. Indeed the very ability of the cultural left to succeed in popularizing cynicism, relativism and suspicion towards big ideas suggests that they were the main beneficiaries of the process of political exhaustion. The ease with which the conservative right crumbled in the Culture War indicated that it had not been able to recover from the setbacks it experienced in previous decades. That this defeat more or less coincided with the demise of the left provided only a few crumbs of comfort. 'Having been spared the class revolution that Marx predicted, we have succumbed to the cultural revolution,' was the bitter verdict of Gertrude Himmelfarb, a leading American conservative thinker.[17]

The verdict of the American sociologist Alan Wolfe on the outcome of the conflicts of the late twentieth century remains pertinent to this day. He remarked that 'the right won the economic war, the left won the cultural war, and the center won the political war'. The different outcomes in these three spheres should not be interpreted as symptoms of a vibrant public life. As we shall see, the main message transmitted by all the contenders is that this is not an age of political truths or alternatives. Public life has become dominated by the fatalism of a politically exhausted centre and not by a contestation of alternatives.

The cumulative impact of the experience of the past seven or eight decades is that it has forced the right to give up on the Past and the left to abandon the hope that it has invested in the Future. Consequently, the remnants of both of these movements are dominated by a profound conformist sensibility towards the present.

Frozen in the present

One of the paradoxes of contemporary times is that although society is dominated by a mood of conformism it finds it difficult to affirm the traditions of the past. Indeed contemporary society appears to be estranged from the legacy of its history. Histories that celebrate a nation's achievement have become marginalized and fallen into disrepute. Old conventions and traditions associated with family life, personal relationships and individual behaviour are denounced for being abusive, cruel, prejudiced, macho or emotionally insensitive. The deferential attitudes of yesterday's hierarchical England is always unfavourably contrasted with today's supposedly inclusive and emotionally literate society. The French Revolution is presented as a precursor of the

Holocaust and America's democratic constitution is sometimes depicted as a charter for slave owners. Attempts to use the traditions of the past as a guide to action in the present are depicted as a malign form of fundamentalism. Social and cultural practices of the past always come with a health warning.

Society's estrangement from its past has led to a situation where traditions have little meaning for everyday life. This demise of tradition deprives conservatives and representatives of the right of very much to uphold. As a result, the numerous attempts to revitalize a conservative movement founded on the celebration of tradition have tended to come unstuck. In response to this loss of history's legacy many so-called conservative modernizers feel uncomfortable with upholding the traditions of the past. They prefer the adoption of 'mild conservatism'. This orientation 'rules out the idea that conservatism can be a mere exercise in nationalistic nostalgia', and this is a further way of calling for the freeing of conservatives from the burden of upholding the traditions of the past.[18] This conservatism is so mild that it is difficult to grasp which values associated with the past it actually wants to conserve.

But, perversely, estrangement from the past coincides with a powerful cultural climate of conservatism. As the Latin American political analyst Norbert Lechner writes, today 'the prevailing slogan is "more of the same"'. He believes that there is 'an increasing concern for conservation – but conservation in relation to nature'.[19] It is worth noting that sections of the so-called Religious Right have adopted environmentalism or 'creation care' as one of their 'values issues'.[20] Consequently, some of the energies that were previously devoted to preserving tradition are now directed at conserving nature. A discernible shift of focus from tradition to the environment represents an attempt to reconcile society's estrangement from its past. But it exacts a high price. It dispossesses people of their history. As Lechner argues, 'the current desire for permanence is no longer based on a consciousness of history'.[21] This is one of the characteristic features of the conservatism of fear. Its imagination is confined to the present and it is no less uncomfortable with the past than it is with the future. Displacing the project of preserving tradition with conserving the present is motivated by a distinctly conformist ethos. Its scorn for the past is combined with a fear of the future.

The right's abandonment of the past is matched by the left's refusal to embrace the future. The left, which has been classically a movement associated with change and progress, has gradually lost its capacity to believe in the future. Throughout most of its existence the left regarded the future as a world that was likely to represent a significant advance over the conditions that prevail. Social change was perceived as, on balance, a positive development and left-wing politics tried to harness it towards the realization of progressive objectives. As a movement oriented towards the future, the present was seen as a condition to be improved, reformed or transformed. Today, the remnant of the left is no less uncomfortable with future prospects than other sections of the political elites.

Contemporary movements associated with the left tend to be particularly uncomfortable with, if not directly hostile to, change. The anti-capitalist and the anti-globalization movements are self-consciously hostile to the ideals that have historically defined the future-oriented left. The legacy of the Enlightenment – reason, progress and universalism – are reviled, and change has become decoupled from the idea of progress. Giddens writes of a world 'where change has long ceased to be all progress'.[22] In a sense it is possible to go a step further and interpret the current disenchantment with change as representing the cultural mood for historical closure. The closure of the historical mind is one of the principal characteristics of today's cultural left.

The left's alienation from the process of change is symptomatic of its internalization of the culture of fear. The intense scepticism regarding the desirability of change reflects its reaction against the idea of progress. There is no perceptible difference in political attitude towards the question of progress: the traditional model of left-wing enthusiasm and right-wing suspicion no longer has much relevance. In the twenty-first century it is difficult to encounter any systematic intellectual defence of progress. If anything, in the recent period suspicion of change is far more marked in the liberal-leftist milieu than anywhere else. The anticipation of catastrophe, particularly ecological, is widespread. This fear of the future is combined with a sense of deference to the present.

Via two very different routes – giving up on the future and losing the past – the left and right have converged on the terrain of the present. A profound sense of presentism pervades the outlook of all sections of the political class. Disconnected from its past and distracted from trying to influence its future, society is afflicted by the enfeeblement of historical consciousness. Projecting the present into the future provides the main frame for conceptualizing change. Lechner hits the nail on the head when he notes that the relationship between past, present and future, through which we try to understand social processes as historic processes, is 'weakened by the overpowering irruption of an omnipresent present'.[23] Frozen in the present, both left and right have lost their distinct characteristics. Political differences and argument are confined to disputes about technical and administrative matters.

How the words lost their meaning

The alienation of politics from the past and from the future deprives its vocabulary of any sense of purpose, perspective and meaning. Frequently, it is unclear what political concepts mean and at any rate they have little in common with their past connotation. There was a time when attitudes towards the Enlightenment played an important role in distinguishing the difference between left and right. The left enthusiastically embraced the Enlightenment ideals of reason, progress and universalism, whilst the right tended to oppose them. Today there is little that divides left from right on this matter. As Bronner notes, the Enlightenment 'is no longer the razor that divides "left" and "right"'. He adds that 'if there is any legitimacy to claims concerning the increasing irrelevance of fundamental political distinctions, indeed, here lies the historical source'.[24]

Take anti-capitalism. The radical critique of capitalism was founded on the premise that this system of production could not systematically develop the productive forces and that therefore it simply could not provide a decent standard of living for all. The claim that capitalism was unable to deliver the goods was frequently presented as an argument for a radically different society by many Socialists and Communists. For the mainstream left, too, capitalism could not be relied on to create the wealth necessary for the maintenance of a prosperous society. In the 1960s and 1970s the left criticized capitalism for causing underdevelopment and serving as an obstacle to the development of societies of the South. Many critics argued that the development of the Third World could not take place along capitalist lines.

The term anti-capitalism today is rarely associated with the claim that this system of production lacks a dynamic towards development. On the contrary, the focus of criticism of radical and left-wing activists is that capitalism develops far too much and far too fast, and that this has destructive consequences for both the environment and for people. The fear today is that there is far too much development and that capitalism produces too many things. 'Today, with its dysfunctional side effects, we are more aware of the dangers; we now experience the inexorable development of productive forces and the global expansion of western civilization more as threats,' argues Jürgen Habermas, a leading German leftist social theorist.[25] If anything, for Habermas capitalism has become much too efficient. 'One can no longer coax an unredeemed promise from the production-centred capitalist project,' he complains.

In direct contrast to the traditions of the nineteenth- and twentieth-century radical movement, those who define themselves as left wing today are weary of economic and technological development. One recent attempt to give some content to the meaning of left wing argued that the orientation towards production was a characteristic feature of the politics of the right. It argued that, 'needless to say, the neo-liberal Right supports the present dominance of the productivist logic, whereas the Left struggles for a shift from the present gross imbalance to a balanced co-existence of the above values/rationalities'.[26]

Apprehension about fast rates of economic growth and the development of new technology is linked to a sense of insecurity regarding change. In what constitutes a dramatic reversal of roles, the left appears to be more uncomfortable in dealing with change than the right. Organizations like the World Social Forum appear more hostile to change than the targets of its criticism. For example, Samir Amin disputes what he calls the 'dominant right wing discourse', which argues that change is always for the better and happens spontaneously. As a result Amin contends that 'we now have to look at what is new in a different way'. He asks 'how can popular forces reorganise to reduce the damage associated with global capitalist expansion?'[27]

Apprehension towards development has been reinterpreted by today's cultural and political elites as a risk. Human progress, once embraced as a wholly desirable enterprise, is today represented as a risk. And a risk is invariably interpreted as a danger to be avoided or minimized. Paradoxically, it is those who call themselves left wing who have become most risk-averse and most vociferous in denouncing the idea of progress. In the nineteenth century, the association of anti-capitalism with hostility to progress was confined to the Luddites and the conservative reaction to modernity. Radicals, liberals and Socialists were for progress. Today, the most bitter opponents of progress are the radical anti-capitalist critics of production and development.

In previous times radical opponents of capitalism denounced the system for failing to provide people with the material possessions they required for a decent life. Today's anti-capitalists believe that we (at least in the West) have too many possessions and reject the 'mindless consumerism' perpetuated by the market. Not surprisingly in an era of 'conspicuous consumption', the problem of poverty has become a less fashionable issue. The term 'child poverty' can still exercise a bit of concern but poverty as such is off the political radar. Not only has the term 'poverty' lost its political meaning, it has also been displaced by the concept of *social exclusion*.

An anti-modernist critique of mass society often lurks behind the label of anti-capitalism. In the first half of the twentieth century, anti-modernist sentiments tended to be linked to the conservative reaction to change. In Europe, conservative thinkers felt uncomfortable with new forms of popular culture and regarded Hollywood, jazz and the crass materialism of the US with dread. Today this response of interwar Little England conservatism is frequently proclaimed by the lifestyle politics of radical activists. Hating MTV, Nike, Coca Cola, McDonald's or Starbucks has become a defining feature of the message. As one advocate of this approach argues, 'attaching political messages to corporate brands becomes a useful way to carry often radical ideas into diverse personal life spaces, as well as across national borders and cultural divides'.[28]

The conservatism of fear disposes both radical critics of the status quo and the upholders of the establishment to become preoccupied with what they see as the mounting dangers facing

human existence. Again, in a reversal of roles, leftist commentators are often more promiscuous in their doom-mongering than
are conservative commentators. They revel in stories about X-
files-style cover-ups over poisoned food, lethal pollutants, new
diseases and other threats to human health. Throughout most of
the past three hundred years conspiracy theories were frequently
used by the right to explain unexpected and unpleasant
developments. Blaming outside agitators, Jewish and Masonic
conspiracies for violent upheavals and disorder was part of the
repertoire of the right-wing political imagination. Today,
conspiracy theory has become appropriated by left-wing commentators. Major events such as the war in Iraq or against
terrorism, as well as the 2004 election of George W. Bush, are
portrayed as the outcome of a plot hatched by a small cabal of
neo-conservatives.

It seems that, regardless of their point of departure,
commentators of different shades of opinion are now likely to
arrive at a strikingly similar conclusion: that the world is an
increasingly dangerous, out-of-control place. All sides promote
the politics of fear. The target of their concern may differ – while
some are anxious about the rise of street crime, others are
obsessed by the variety of abuses that children face. The right is
apprehensive about the threat of terrorism, the left is anxious
about some impending environmental catastrophe. What seems
to divide political figures is what and how they should fear.

What's left?

Many of the ideas usually associated with the right in the
nineteenth century – fear of progress, of science, of modernity
and of collective action – are today closely linked with the
outlook of left-wing thinkers. Friedrich Nietzsche, the philosopher of the right at the turn of the twentieth century, is now

fashionable among the cultural left and postmodernist intelligentsia. As Stephen Bronner notes in his important study *Reclaiming the Enlightenment*, 'ideas long associated with reactionary movements – the privileging of experience over reason, national or ethnic identity over internationalism … the community over the individual, custom over innovation, myth over science – have entered the thinking of the American left'.[29] The political scientist Brian Barry agrees. He argues that 'during most of the nineteenth and twentieth centuries, attitudes to the Enlightenment marked the main division between left and right'. But now the right's critique of the Enlightenment has 'gained currency among those who see themselves as being on the left'.[30] Hostility to universalist values is most pronounced among the cultural left.

This is not just a change in taste: it is a testimony to the fact that in many respects the distinction between left and right has lost its meaning. In this topsy-turvy world the so-called right-wing thinker is sometimes more progressive or at least more future oriented than his left-wing counterpart. At least some of them are trying – albeit unsuccessfully – to uphold a semblance of rationality and to promote universal values. It is among the left-wing intelligentsia that the greatest scorn is reserved for the ideas of progress associated with the Enlightenment. Thus it is not simply the possibility but also the desirability of social change that is now being questioned by the left/liberal intelligentsia.

The occasional attempt to resurrect the distinction between left and right shows how irrelevant these terms have become. The Italian political philosopher Norbert Bobbio has written a short book that is designed to argue the case for the enduring relevance of the left and right distinction. Bobbio argues that the difference between 'left and right mainly concerns values'. He claims that the two are distinguished by the right's adherence to tradition and the left's embrace of emancipation.[31] Whilst this representation of the difference between left and right may have had some relevance in the past it fails to capture the contemporary reality.

As we noted earlier, the right no longer feels comfortable with upholding tradition and the left has abandoned its belief in emancipation.

One way that Bobbio attempts to uphold the distinction between left and right is through the process of logical deduction. 'As the centre is defined as neither left-wing nor right-wing and cannot be defined in any other way, its very existence and *raison d'être* are based on this antithesis.'[32] The argument that if there is a centre there must be a left or right depends on geometry rather than political life for its evidence. In previous times, centrism often sought to establish a consensus that incorporated the demands of left and right. This was a centrism – for example, the consensus politics of the UK in the 1950s – that defined itself in relation to the left and the right. Today, centrist projects such as the Third Way define themselves not against left or right but against politics. Centrism today is a self-consciously anti-political project adhering to the dogma of 'there is no alternative'.

Bobbio seems to believe that as long as there is political conflict it must be underpinned by the classical differentiation between left and right. However, when politics is emptied of content conflicts often have an arbitrary character. Who would have imagined that gun ownership in the US and fox hunting in the UK would be issues that would distinguish left from right? The attempt to find remnants of a distinct political outlook increasingly assumes the character of an exercise in ideological excavation. Take the case of the leftist author of *So Now Who Do We Vote For?*, who desperately sought to discover living political issues that could add up to a coherent leftist alternative. It is a sign of the times that the formula he arrived at was to take a stand against the war in Iraq, 'the iniquities of tuition fees and Foundation Hospitals'.[33] This artificial weaving together of three disparate issues is so unconvincing that even its author cannot justify it without striking a note of embarrassment. Increasingly, the question 'what do we stand for?' provokes responses that are both rhetorical and banal. A well-known New Labour journalist asks why her Party's leaders are so reluctant about spelling out their distinct values. 'They know what those values are: it's public versus the private realm, opportunity not privilege, politics that puts family before business and gives children a chance,' she exclaims.[34] In political terms, taking a stand on the public, the family and children represents a roundabout way of acknowledging the absence of distinct values.

Even issues that are hotly debated appear to be disembedded from wider political conflicts. It seems to me that heated controversies frequently involve single-issue campaigns that self-consciously eschew wider political affiliations. In the US so-called 'values issues' are not reducible to party politics. Republican hardliner Dick Cheney opposed Bush on same-sex marriage. Arnie campaigned for public funding for stem-cell research – as did Mrs Nancy Reagan. And the Republican Party made a big fuss of courting the Hispanic vote in the name of diversity, running Spanish language ads in the South-West and Florida. Movements demanding gun-control, the abolition of animal experimentation, an end to abortion, new rights for ethnic groups or same-sex marriage are not seeking to build a new political system and are not in the business of offering an alternative to the status quo. Often, as in the case of the Social Forums, protest movements eschew the politics of 'big ideas' and regard politics with suspicion.

Still, commentators find it very difficult to let go of the categories of left and right. Bronner argues that 'political theory cannot help but distinguish left from right'. Why? Because 'it was the liberal political theory of the Enlightenment' which 'generated the division between left and right in the first place'. Yet, Bronner himself argues persuasively that attitudes towards the Enlightenment no longer distinguish left from right and that support for its legacy is conspicuous by its weakness. It is time to acknowledge that the distinction between left and right has ceased to have practical consequences. Wherever one stands on the traditional spectrum of politics, it is time to consider leaving behind the Palaeolithic categories of left and right.

Often the call to go 'beyond left and right' represents the demand to give up on politics altogether. Sometimes it expresses the aspiration to restrain the ambitions associated with the politics of the Enlightenment. My call to recognize the irrelevance of these categories is motivated by a very different impulse. It is motivated by the goal of getting rid of the distractions that confuse contemporary public life. Of course people are entitled to call themselves whatever they choose. But the differences that really matter today are fundamentally about where one stands in relation to the past and the future. Those who are interested in the restoration of politics need to rework society's relation to the past and adopt a more activist orientation to the future. But the realization of this objective requires the promotion of a more robust sensibility towards the human potential. Addressing this issue is the subject of the next chapter.

4 Deference to Fate

It is tempting to blame the current state of political stasis on the behaviour of politicians, their parties or an irresponsible media. However, the problems discussed in this book are not the direct outcome of any specific errors or conscious strategy. They are the by-product of the growth of popular disenchantment and disbelief in the promise of modernity. One important dimension of twenty-first-century fatalism relevant for making sense of the disenchantment with politics is the tendency to question the capacity of people to possess the wisdom both to understand and shape their circumstances. Such a pessimistic cultural account of the relationship between people and the making of history has important implications for the way that the life of politics is experienced. Perversely, political commentators often write of the end of deference.[1] What they overlook is that the decline of deference to traditional authority has been replaced by a far more powerful sense of deference to Fate.

Political analysts frequently draw attention to the decline of the politics of class and of the politics of community. However, this erosion of previous forms of solidarity is paralleled by a far more important and fundamental process – the loss of the belief that people can shape or alter their circumstances through political action. Instead of perceiving themselves as political subjects, individuals frequently experience their role as the objects of policy making. The process of *declining subjectivity* has intensified the sense of powerlessness and passivity of the public. It is a form of self-consciousness which is even evident when citizens react against their alienation from the political system. Such reactions often assume the form of a demand for an apology, compensation, recognition or affirmation. This response often resembles that of a disenchanted customer rather than a public-interest-oriented citizen.

The consciousness of powerlessness or what sociologists describe as a *loss of agency* is continually fuelled by cultural forces that heighten the sense of fatalism. As noted in our discussion on the freezing of history, a mood prevails that discourages the idea that people can, by interacting with each other and their circumstances, shape their own destinies. Instead of acting as agents of history, humanity has effectively been recast in the role of an object to which things happen by forces that are beyond all control. The assumption of numerous policy documents is that people are not trustworthy and cannot be expected to live their lives responsibly. The tendency to treat adults as children informs the action of the entire political class. Individuals are no longer presented as the 'political man' or even as 'citizens'. Today's political vocabulary emphasizes the passivity and powerlessness of the public. We have the excluded, the vulnerable (potential victim), the victim, the bullied, the client, the end user, the consumer or the stakeholder, but not people as political animals.

The infantalization of the electorate is assisted by social processes that have served to disconnect people from one another. The increasing fragmentation of social experience has had a significant impact on people's lives, helping to normalize a more privatized and individuated way of living. Some commentators claim that this more privatized existence has encouraged the development of a thrusting individual consciousness, of the kind they now associate with the 'greedy eighties'. But they could not be more wrong. Without known points of contact and a reliable system of support, individuation only encourages powerlessness. The sense of being on your own and of having to rely on individual solutions has only led to a heightened consciousness of isolation. It has had the effect of altering the way that people see their relationship with the world, helping to induce an exaggerated sense of weakness and a fatalistic outlook. The finding of numerous surveys that people expect their future to be worse than the present is symptomatic of this trend. So is the powerful tendency continually to emphasize the negative side of every new development.

The heightened sense of individual insecurity that prevails today tends to fluctuate between passivity and a sporadic outburst of anxiety of the kind that characterizes public reaction to MMR, global warming or the threat of terrorism. The coincidence of social passivity with outbursts of anxiety has helped to endow political action with a peculiarly timid bias. Today's causes tend to be about the politics of survival – global warming, AIDS, saving our food from contamination.

The growth of individual insecurity is a by-product of a fundamental alteration in the relation between the individual and society. Individual attitudes are mediated through a complex of institutions and relations; classes and communities have provided an important experience through which individuals make sense of the world. Over the past three centuries people's experience of modernity through these institutions has served to widen their horizons and helped forge a sense of human agency. The development of individual ambition and of a class- or community-based vision of social change often expressed outwardly contradictory aspirations. But their differences notwithstanding, what such responses had in common was a perception of future possibilities, and the belief that human action could make a difference.

Today, this human-centred view of the world has been replaced by one in which the range of possible options has been severely narrowed. This is strikingly expressed in the domain of politics, where even the capacity of the state to give direction to society is increasingly called into question. Politics matters less to people for the very simple reason that what people can do does not appear to matter. The sense of impotence often takes on the form of attacking politics itself. Anti-politics, the cynical dismissal of the elected politician and the obsession with sleaze and corruption, expresses a deeply cynical view of the human experience. This orientation renounces the history-making potential of people on the grounds that trying to do something either makes no difference or makes matters worse. If this was simply a case of saying that there is no point voting for any of today's parties, it would be fair enough. But the current disparagement of politics goes way beyond that. The conviction that we cannot trust politics is ultimately a roundabout way of saying that we cannot trust anybody – and that includes ourselves.

Pouring scorn on political ambition is not simply motivated by scepticism regarding the efficacy of participation and engagement. It is also informed by the conviction that the pursuit of ambition is likely to end in tears. In the nineteenth century, people were criticized for not knowing their place. Today they are castigated for not knowing their natural limits and encouraged to defer to Fate.

The construction of the vulnerable citizen

The culture of fatalism does not merely call into question the efficacy of political action. Through redefining the very meaning of personhood, it also calls into question the ability of the individual to assume a political role. A powerful sense of powerlessness is communicated when people indicate that they do not think that their political involvement can make a difference. Often this sense of powerlessness is blamed on the unresponsiveness of politicians and the inflexibility of political institutions.

For example, the disengagement of young people from the political process is repeatedly presented as the result of the failure of central government to listen to them. One researcher upholding this thesis notes that 'there is a very strong sense among our respondents that they are marginalized or excluded from political decision-making or debates'.[2] It appears that the respondents indicated that they perceived politics as 'something that is done to them, not something they can influence'. There is little doubt that politicians and governments are often unresponsive to the electorate and that many people feel marginalized and excluded from public institutions. But as noted before, the unresponsive character of political institutions cannot account for the loss of the sense of agency. In previous circumstances, unresponsive institutions have provoked protest and revolt. And history provides many examples of situations where citizens organized and used political pressure to force the powers that be to listen to them.

To understand the sense of powerlessness that pervades public life it is necessary to look at the way contemporary culture influences the way we regard ourselves as human beings. The prevailing sense of diminished subjectivity is underwritten by a distinct code about the workings of human behaviour and personhood. Every culture provides a set of ideas and beliefs about the nature of human beings and what constitutes their personhood. Our ideas about what we can expect from one another, how we handle uncertainty and change, how we deal with adversity and pain, and how we view history are underpinned by the particular account that a culture offers about personhood and the human potential. As I argue elsewhere, the defining feature of the current Western twenty-first-century version of personhood is its *vulnerability*.[3] Although society still upholds the ideals of self-determination and autonomy, the values associated with them are increasingly overridden by a more dominant message that stresses the quality of human weakness.

What I have called elsewhere *therapy culture* casts serious doubts about the capacity of the self to manage new challenges and to cope with adversity.[4] Individuals confronted with the ordinary troubles of life are now routinely advised to seek professional advice and counselling. The belief that people exist in a state of vulnerability informs the way that we are expected to make sense of our experiences. As a cultural metaphor, vulnerability is used to highlight the claim that people and their communities lack the emotional and psychological resources necessary to deal with change and make choices. This metaphor also suggests that people do not possess the emotional resources to deal with adversity. Popular culture, too, encourages the view that communities and people are weak and in need of support.

The term 'vulnerability' is habitually used as if it is a permanent feature of a person's biography. It is presented and experienced as a natural state of being that shapes human response. It is a label that describes entire groups in society. That is why it has become common to use the recently constructed concept of *vulnerable groups*. The term 'vulnerable group' does not simply refer to groups of the psychologically distraught or to a small minority of economically insecure individuals. Children, indeed all children, are automatically assumed to be vulnerable. A study of the emergence of the concept of vulnerable children shows that in most published literature, the concept is treated as 'a relatively self-evident concomitant of childhood which requires little formal exposition'. It is a taken-for-granted idea that is rarely elaborated on: 'children are considered vulnerable as individuals by definition, through both their physical and other perceived immaturities'. Moreover this state of vulnerability is presented as an intrinsic attribute. It is 'considered to be an *essential* property of individuals, as something which is intrinsic to children's identities and personhoods, and which is recognisable through their beliefs and actions, or indeed through just their appearance'.[5] However, it is not just children who are defined as vulnerable *en masse*. So are women, the elderly, ethnic minorities, the disabled and the poor. Indeed, if all the groups designated as vulnerable by experts and policy makers are added together it would appear that they constitute nearly 100 per cent of the population!

Take the following advertisement for the post of Adult Protection Coordinator. 'Protecting and empowering vulnerable adults is a priority in Greenwich,' states the ad for the post by Greenwich Council in South London.[6] The ad effortlessly transmits the idea that there is indeed a category of people called 'vulnerable adults' and that they require the protection of a paid professional. The ideals of child protection are imported into the provision of services for adults. As we argue in Chapter 8, this ethos of infantilization is one of the strongest drivers of public policy. Vulnerability works as a cultural metaphor rather than as a precise concept. Its meaning is far from clear, it being used to describe people's experience of a wide variety of phenomena. The promoters of this metaphor rarely ask the question 'vulnerable to what?' For the only answer provoked by this question is 'vulnerable to everything'. So vulnerability does not exist in relation to a specific event or experience. It is a diagnosis of the human condition that perpetually encourages a sense of deference to Fate.

The sense of vulnerability is so deeply immersed in our cultural imagination that it is easy to overlook the fact that it is a relatively recently invented concept. The term 'vulnerable group' did not exist in the 1970s – it came into usage in the 80s. One study notes that the tendency to frame children's problems through the metaphor of vulnerability became visible in the late 80s but took off in the 1990s.[7] The timing of the ascendancy of this way of interpreting human experience is important as it coincides with the triumph of the idea of TINA. This is not surprising, since once people are consigned to lead a life of vulnerability their capacity to choose an alternative becomes compromised.

Through the paradigm of vulnerability, the sense of powerlessness is cultivated as part of the normal state of being. The sense of powerlessness assigned to the contemporary self is unprecedented in the age of modernity. The emphasis on human vulnerability dooms people to the role of helpless victims of circumstances. The converse of this deflation of the status of human subjectivity is the inflation of the threat that external circumstances represent to the integrity of the individual self. The vulnerability and impotence of the individual stands in sharp contrast to the formidable powers attributed to the everyday challenges that people confront. The self-determining or history-making role of people is all but abolished in this representation of the relationship between humanity and the process of change. Through the constant amplification of the risks facing humanity – pollution, global warming, weapons of mass destruction, catastrophic flu epidemic, and a large variety of other health scares – even the limited exercise of individual choice becomes restricted by the harsh regime of uncertainty.

The model of human vulnerability and powerlessness is transmitted through powerful ideas that call into question people's capacity to assume a measure of control over their affairs. Social commentators regularly declare that we live in the era of the 'death of the subject', 'death of the author', 'decentred subject', 'end of history' or 'end of politics'. Such pessimistic accounts of the human potential inform both intellectual and cultural life in the West. They provide cultural legitimation for the downsizing of the idea of the active citizen.

The survivalist outlook that characterizes the vulnerable individual is also shaped by the conviction that the world has become an intensely dangerous place beyond the control of people. Society is continually haunted by the expectation of crisis and catastrophe. Environmental disasters, weapons of mass destruction, 'technology gone mad' are just some of the concerns that have helped to fashion a permanent sense of crisis.

The relationship between the individual sense of vulnerability and the wider global threats to human existence is most clearly represented through the concept of being 'at risk'. The conceptualization of being 'at risk' is again a relatively recent invention that is bound up with the emergence of the ethos of 'there is no alternative'. Its entry into the vernacular coincides with the consolidation of the mood of political exhaustion. The concept of being at risk encapsulates an outlook which is dramatically different from the classical notion of taking a risk. The formulation 'to take a risk' contains the assumption that individuals can both exercise choice and choose to explore and experiment. Taking a risk has as its premise active subjects whose actions have the potential to realize positive outcomes and exercise a degree of control over their circumstances. In contrast, the concept of being at risk reverses the previous relationship between human beings and experience. To be at risk assigns to the person a passive and dependent role. It is no longer about what you do but about who you are – acknowledgement of powerlessness, at least in relation to that risk. Increasingly, someone defined as being at risk is seen to exist in a permanent condition of vulnerability. The term objectifies the vulnerability of the self. At risk has become the fixed attribute of individuals.

Being at risk implies the autonomy of the dangers that people face. It also reverses the idea of the autonomous subject acting on the world so that it is the objectified self that is acted upon. Being at risk annihilates the possibility of choice. In this scenario, the risks are the active agents and people at risk are cast into the role of passivity and unbounded vulnerability.

Agency panic

Our culture's version of the diminished self is part of a wider reaction to the promise of modernity. Strong anti-modernist sentiments question the ideal of human progress. In its most systematic form, this scepticism has turned into an anti-humanist worldview that is cynical about the potential that men and women possess for influencing their destiny. This belittling of the human potential has as its premise the belief that the attempt by humans to control their destiny is not only unrealistic but also very dangerous. Values and forms of behaviour that are linked to risk taking, experimentation or the project of assuming mastery over one's destiny are frequently castigated as a negative form of behaviour. Such sentiments enjoy little cultural support. Instead they are rejected as symptoms of arrogant and destructive behaviour by irresponsible humans. The assertion of self-determination and the attempt to control the future course of events is depicted as the precursor to destructive outcomes. Such negative sentiments are often directed at the ambition to control nature, which is regularly criticized for causing many of the environmental problems facing the world.

The tendency to denigrate the idea of self-determination reflects a potent mood of disenchantment towards the experience of human progress during the past century. Not only is the ideal of individual self-determination regarded with scepticism, but contemporary culture provides little support for the idea of societal self-determination. Both individually and collectively, people are assumed to lack the capacity to assume control over societal forces. These assumptions are conveyed through influential theories of *risk society*, which depict the world as if it is threatened by a semi-conscious humanity that is desperately attempting to negotiate the forces – mainly destructive – that it has created. According to this model, powerless human agents who confront powerful forces have no choice but to engage in an exercise of damage limitation. Ulrich Beck echoes this point in his book on the subject: 'basically, one is no longer concerned with attaining something "good" but rather with preventing the worst'.[8]

The perception that the world is an increasingly out-of-control place leads to the pursuit of damage limitation as the sensible response towards the experience of change. That is why *the fear of change* constitutes such an important theme in current deliberations about the problems that will face us in the future. This motif of fear driving people's response to social experience has gained cultural credibility. It is justified on the ground that we are entitled to be scared since risks that we experience today are unbounded. This perception of risk is rooted in the sense of unbounded vulnerability transmitted through therapeutic culture. The world does become more dangerous when the self is perceived to be uniquely powerless and vulnerable. The relationship between the vulnerable subject and the changing world is mediated through a consciousness of risk permeated by fear. Risk consciousness and the perception of emotional vulnerability can be interpreted as integral to the fatalistic cultural orientation that underpins the ethos of no alternative. Cultural fatalism renders a wholly pessimistic account of the capacity for human control and reasoning.

Since the eighteenth century, critics of the Enlightenment have always questioned the capacity for human reasoning. In the nineteenth century such anti-humanist opponents of modernity claimed that 'irrational' and 'unconscious' forces tend to be more powerful than that of reason.[9] Since then such anti-modernist reactions have emerged periodically to call into question the status of science and reason. During the 1980s this trend acquired significant momentum. And from this period onwards, the tendency to restrain the status of reason has become a dominant feature of Western intellectual life. Even in academic circles rationality is assigned a far more modest role than in the nineteenth century. Disappointment with the experience of modernity has generated a mood of doubt towards the authority of reason. The sociologist Jeffrey Alexander writes of the 'omnipresence of irrationality'. According to Alexander, reason 'has been experienced as a hollow shell, progress as inconceivable, and often actually undesirable'.[10]

One reason why rationality is sometimes represented as undesirable is because it seems to be responsible for many of the ills confronting society. The Enlightenment and its vision of progress and rationality has been blamed for mass destruction, the rise of totalitarianism and the Holocaust. The association of science and technology with frightening and dreadful outcomes has become commonplace in both intellectual and cultural life. Films such as *The Day After Tomorrow, Independence Day*, or *Armageddon* indict the presumption of an 'arrogant' science and scientist for 'playing God' and inadvertently unleashing powers of mass destruction. Such attitudes towards the development of science and knowledge are not confined to Hollywood. Many of the leading authorities on the sociology of risk associate the new dangers facing the world with the advance of knowledge. They argue that many of the uncertainties and anxieties that we face are the result of the growth of human knowledge.[11] In turn, the mood of growing uncertainty has the effect of distracting individuals from making meaningful choices.

The association of knowledge with danger has an important influence on the way that people make sense of the world. Critics of the authority of science hold the pursuit of knowledge responsible for setting in motion innovations whose development is likely to have unintended destructive consequences. The expectation that we cannot predict the outcome of our actions strengthens uncertainty and encourages a negative interpretation of future events. Lack of knowledge and the sentiment that it is not possible to know weakens the human capacity to initiate and experiment. It even creates a climate that encourages people to regard knowledge and the products of knowledge as risky if not dangerous.

Frequently, the dangers faced by the human species are represented as ones that we can't really understand. In contrast to the Enlightenment's conviction that knowledge could eventually solve all problems, the intellectual temper of our times is hospitable to views that insist on the impossibility of knowing. Such a pessimistic account of the capacity to understand has important implications for how society views its future. If the consequences of our actions for the future are not knowable, then our anxieties towards change become amplified. This scepticism about our inability to anticipate outcomes is often based on the argument that we simply do not have the time to catch up with the fast and far-reaching consequences of modern technological development. Many experts claim that since the consequences of technological innovations are realized so swiftly, there is simply no time to understand their likely effects. According to the German social scientist Niklas Luhmann, the absence of time required to obtain necessary information weakens hope in rationality.[12]

The devaluation of people's capacity to know has a significant influence on the way that people make sense of the world around them. Once knowledge is deprived of authority, people lose an important instrument for interpreting events. Without the guidance of knowledge, world events can appear as random and arbitrary acts beyond comprehension. Not surprisingly, social and political life is experiencing a *crisis of causality*. A crisis of causality does not simply deprive society from grasping the chain of events that has led to a particular outcome. It also diminishes the capacity to find meaning in what sometimes appears as a series of patternless events. In contemporary times, making sense of contemporary events is proving particularly troublesome. In such circumstances knowledge helps little to assist us in gaining meaning about events. That is why official knowledge about the death of Diana, the reason for the US invasion of Iraq, 9/11, the shortage of flu vaccines during the 2004 US Presidential elections, and the power blackout on both sides of the Atlantic in 2003 are treated with scepticism by significant sections of the public.

Society's crisis of causality leads many to seek explanations in the realm of conspiracies. Indeed, the growing influence of conspiracy theories over the public imagination is one of the most remarkable manifestations of the contemporary sense of diminished subjectivity. The embrace of conspiracy theories is often motivated by a sense of incomprehension towards the workings of the world. According to one account, 'a conspiracy theory typically claims that there is a hidden agenda and a hidden hand behind current events'. Such theories provide an alternative to knowledge based on a grasp of the causes of events. 'In effect conspiracy theories have tended to restore a sense of agency, causality and responsibility to what would otherwise seem the inexplicable play of forces over which we have no control,' argues Peter Knight in his exploration of the relationship between our heightened sense of risk and the rise of conspiracy theories.[13]

The loss of a sense of causality has encouraged perceptions that associate negative and destructive episodes with intentional malevolent behaviour. Such episodes are frequently blamed on the self-serving purposeful acts of politicians, public and business figures, doctors, scientists – indeed all professionals. One of the most important ways in which the sense of diminished subjectivity is experienced is the feeling that the individual is manipulated and influenced by hidden powerful forces: not just spin-doctors, subliminal advertising and the media, but also powers that have no name. That is why we frequently attribute unexplained physical and psychological symptoms to unspecific forces caused by the food we eat, the water we drink, an extending variety of pollutants and substances transmitted by new technologies, and other invisible processes. The American academic Timothy Melley has characterized this response as *agency panic*. 'Agency panic is intense anxiety about an apparent loss of autonomy, the conviction that one's actions are being controlled by someone else or that one has been "constructed" by powerful, external agents,' writes Melley.[14] The perception that one's behaviour and actions are controlled by external agents is symptomatic of a heightened sense of fatalism that is associated with the sense of diminished subjectivity. The feeling of being subject to manipulation and external control – the very stuff of conspiracy theory – is a sensibility that is consistent with the perception of being vulnerable or 'at risk'. As Melley observed, this reaction 'stems largely from a sense of *diminished human agency*, a feeling that individuals cannot effect meaningful social action and, in extreme cases, may not be able to control their own behaviour'.[15]

The revitalization of pre-modern anxieties about the workings of hidden forces is a testimony to a weakening of the humanist sensibility that emerged as part of the Enlightenment. The loss of a sense of human agency has not only undermined the public's engagement with politics, it has also altered the way that people make sense of the world around them. The crisis of causality is experienced as a world where most important events are shaped and determined by a hidden agenda. We seem to be living in a shadowy world akin to *The Matrix Trilogy*, where the issues at stake are the reality that we inhabit and who is being manipulated by whom. In previous times, such attitudes mainly informed the thinking of right-wing populist movements, which saw the hand of a Jewish, Masonic or Communist conspiracy behind major world events. Today, conspiracy theory has become mainstream and many of its most vociferous supporters are to be found in radical protest movements and amongst the cultural left. When Hillary Clinton warned of a 'vast Right Wing Conspiracy' it became evident that the politics of the hidden agenda has been internalized into everyday public life. Today, the anti-capitalist, anti-globalization movement is no less wedded to the politics of conspiracy than its opponents on the far right. From their perspective a vast global neo-conservative conspiracy has turned into an all-purpose explanation for the many ills that afflict our times.

The simplistic worldview of conspiracy thinking helps fuel suspicion and mistrust towards the domain of politics. It displaces a critical engagement with public life with a destructive search for the hidden agenda. It distracts from the clarification of genuine differences and helps turn public life into a theatre where what matters are the private lives and personal interests of mistrusted politicians. In turn, the media fuels this attitude by transmitting the belief that what is important is not what public figures actually say but what is their 'real' agenda. It incites the public to look for hidden motives. No one is as they seem. This normalization of suspicion and mistrust does not possess any critical dimension. Agency panic represents the fear that the vulnerable subject bears towards an incomprehensible changing world. There really is no alternative – only Fate!

5 The Conformist Revolt Against History

Although bookshops are stocked mile high with historical biographies and texts, Western society feels surprisingly uncomfortable with its history. This loss of historical imagination is the flip-side of the tendency to defer to Fate.

Anxiety towards change

Not surprisingly, the fatalistic mood of 'there is no alternative' continually fuels anxieties concerning the future. The separation of human agency from the making of history is based on a form of consciousness that regards change as a random potentially destructive process that is likely to result in a more dangerous world. The overriding theme of contemporary public life is the fear of change. It is difficult to think of any film, novel or other production of art which depicts the future in positive terms. In recent decades science fiction has become indistinguishable from the horror film. The fear of change also has a deep popular resonance. The vision of humanity, helpless in the face of a variety of environmental disasters, highlights our deep-seated apprehensions about the future. Speculation that the December 2004 tsunami that devastated parts of Asia was caused by aliens from space who wanted to realign the world's rotation competes with statements made by respectable scientists who suggest that we should be aware of the potential threat from an asteroid-caused tsunami.[1]

In previous times, uncertainty about the future coincided with the tendency to romanticize the past. Nostalgia for the 'Good Old Days' and the celebration of the achievements of the past indicated ambivalence towards change and an uncertain future. Appeals to the authority of tradition constituted an implicit warning against breaking with the practices of the past. Nostalgia for the past continues to represent an important theme in popular culture. However, this idealization of a Golden Age has been forced onto the defensive by a far more powerful tendency to denigrate yesteryear. Typically today, the past is packaged with a health warning too.

As noted previously, in recent times the appeal of tradition has diminished. Today we are less inclined to celebrate the legacy and achievements of the past. Moreover, past traditions no longer confer automatic authority on individuals and institutions. In popular culture the 'Good Old Days' are often portrayed as an era that possessed few redeeming features. Instead of achievements we dwell on the themes of human cruelty, oppression and trauma. Popular fiction and television are far more likely to dwell on the Bad Old Days than to idealize the past.

The tendency to pathologize the past does not mean that it has ceased to play an important role in contemporary culture. However, it is used in ways that are quite distinct from previous practice. Today, the past is mobilized to call into question human ambition. Accounts of the past seek to reinterpret humanity's achievements over the centuries through a distinctly negative frame. Previous flattering accounts of human endeavour and achievement are giving way to stories written by authors fascinated with the dark side of history. Those devoted to the twenty-first-century project of plundering the past are preoccupied with excavating its atrocities and horrors. Their preoccupation is with reinterpreting the past as a story of human abuse, atrocity, genocide, ethnic cleansing and, of course, numerous Holocausts. In his study of the relationship between the

Holocaust and German national identity, Bernhard Giesen argues that 'in contrast to classical modernity and the universalistic patterns of identity associated with it, the new pattern of identity is based not on the attractiveness of the future but on the horrors of the past'. And he adds that today 'the horror of the past and the remembrance of the victims replace the attraction of utopias that once produced the victims'.[2] A morose fascination with human evil – the paedophile, the serial killer, the terrorist – threatens to overwhelm our capacity to imagine an individual's potential for altruism, heroism or simply doing good. The shift of focus from the historical hero to the victim-survivor of history mirrors the trend towards the emergence of the vulnerable form of subjectivity that we discussed in the last chapter.

During the past two centuries, the key motif in the rewriting of history was the desire to promote the unique greatness of a particular people or culture. National myths were about heroic deeds and glorious events. Such myths were not simply used as sentimental celebrations of the past. They were mobilized to construct a positive vision of the future. The myth of the American frontier promised a great destiny for that society. British, French and German national myths were mobilized to provide an optimistic representation of these cultures' future. Today, the rewriting of history is driven by a very different impulse. The manipulation of collective memory makes no grand claims on the future. On the contrary, the historic memory serves as a monument to a people's historic suffering. Its focus is on the destructive side of the human species. 'If we people did such awful things to one another in the past why should we expect anything positive from them in the future?' is the message that is implicit in the new genre of anti-humanist history.

The tendency to regard the past as the history of victimization and brutalization where every previous generation contributes to making the world an even more dangerous place than the one before, serves as a reminder against the ambition of human agency. Virtually every influential cultural movement today is complicit in rewriting the past as a story of human cruelty and degradation. History is being recycled as a cautionary tale against the aspiration to exercise human subjectivity. According to one account, 'the birth of ecological awareness, feminist conscious-ness, or the concept of universal human rights makes everybody see the conquest of nature, gender oppression, and other inequalities and injustices in a completely new light'.[3] Through reading history backwards, society accounts for its sense of disorientation as the consequence of the destructive acts of human history.

The continuous serving up of the horrors of the past has as its purpose the demand for lowering human ambition. It main consequence is to freeze history in the present. This sentiment is systematically expressed by the culturally dominant standpoint of the conservatism of fear. The project of freezing history in the present makes perfect sense from the perspective of 'there is no alternative'. If there is indeed no alternative, preserving the status quo becomes the principal duty of society. Of course there is nothing particularly novel or distinct about the aspiration for permanence. But today, this desire for permanence represents an attempt to close off society both from its past and from its future. It is a form of presentism that directly negates historical thinking. As Lechner remarks, 'the current desire for permanence is no longer based on a consciousness of history'.[4]

Historical thinking

Without historical thinking, politics turns into a caricature of itself. It is when people possess the capacity to think historically that they can begin to see that their actions can have a significant bearing on their circumstance. Historical thinking is a form of consciousness oriented towards altering the human condition. It regards all social arrangements as transient, and therefore susceptible to further improvement through the way people negotiate the challenges they face. During the past three centuries, historical thinking directly encouraged the construction of political alternatives to the status quo. The claim that such alternatives have become irrevocably exhausted constitutes the root of the sense of malaise that afflicts twenty-first-century politics.

Historical thinking represents one of the greatest achievements of the Enlightenment tradition. It recognizes and affirms the transformative dynamic of human action, especially in its future-oriented and culturally purposeful form. The early eighteenth-century humanist thinker Giambattista Vico was one of the first to grasp the responsibility of human beings for the making of history:

> In the night of thick darkness enveloping the earliest antiquity, so remote from ourselves, there shines the eternal and never-failing light of a truth beyond all question: that the world of civil society has certainly been made by man, and that its principles are therefore to be found within the modifications of our human mind.[5]

The sense of history making as a defining feature of the human condition led Vico and others to endow this activity with an essentially positive character.

With the emergence of historical thinking, the sense of change became theorized for the first time. Change itself became an issue, the premier intellectual problem of the time. This sense of change was closely linked to the recognition that human subjectivity was not external to, but part of, history. A new sense of temporality gave human consciousness a decisive role in the shaping of history. Such sentiments directly contradict the temper of our times. Today, terms like naive, arrogant and pernicious are used to dismiss Vico's view of how history is made. In particular, the role of reason and human consciousness is assigned a marginal role in history making.

The attempt to make sense of the present and interpret the future in accordance with a system of ideas is sometimes denounced as ideological, fanatical, utopian or millenarian. Critics of historical thinking share the premise that human beings have little control over their actions and still less over the outcome. As today, former critics of reason believed that the impotence of human agency limited the scope for the exercise of subjectivity. The liberal critic Friedrich Hayek insisted that men and women were always the objects, but never the subjects, of history. 'Man is not and never will be the master of his fate: his very reason progresses by leading him into the unknown and unforeseen where he learns new things.' Despite his pessimistic account of human agency, Hayek still offered a positive view, in which humanity progresses and learns, albeit in unforeseen and unexpected circumstances. In contrast, contemporary critics of reason and progress go much further, and even stigmatize the humanist aspiration for expanding the frontier of knowledge.[6]

Regardless of their philosophical or political differences, until recently most serious thinkers believed that there were important lessons that could be learned from history. Those disposed towards a conservative outlook went so far as to claim that the traditions of the past could convey transcendental truths relevant to people for all times. Others drew different lessons and regarded history as an inspiration for showing the possibility for progressive change. Today's conservatism of fear adopts a very different approach. As far as it is concerned, the past possesses no truth as such but an indictment of those who seek it. The consequence of this orientation is not confined to the question of how we view former times. Irresponsibility towards the past encourages the tendency to incite panic concerning the future.

The denigration of the human subject

Society's estrangement from its past creates circumstances in which classical political distinctions and divisions make little sense. The fundamental questions that have divided left and right since the eighteenth century pale into insignificance compared to the issue of what it means to be human. Previous political foes on the left and right – despite their differences – all drew something positive from the experience of human history making. Scientific and progressive thought have always recognized that preserving the achievements of the past is a precondition for moving forward in a positive direction. 'If I have seen further it is by standing on the shoulders of giants,' observed Sir Isaac Newton. For conservative thinkers the past is an important source of enlightenment. They regard tradition as possessing the capacity to confer wisdom and insight on human action in the present. Both perspectives view civilization in essentially positive terms and use the word without a sense of embarrassment.

Although the conservative and progressive views of the past were informed by fundamentally different perspectives they both affirmed the importance of embracing aspects of human experience. The differences that existed on this issue between the two traditions are negligible compared to the chasm that separates them from the contemporary anti-humanist rendering of the past. The devaluation of the past and its transformation into a horror story encourages a sense of utter purposelessness, and alienation from a sense of humanity.

Confronting the culture of fatalism requires an alliance between all those who uphold the unique character of the human. Such a project will no doubt involve surprising and unexpected bedfellows. As the literary critic Terry Eagleton argues, political opponents have a common interest in upholding the gains of the Enlightenment. He claims that Marxists 'recognize that there can be no authentic socialism without the rich heritage of enlightened bourgeois liberalism'.[7] There is a common heritage of enlightened thought that needs to be preserved and taken forward by all those who possess a humanist instinct. For now, standing up for the legacy of civilization needs to transcend the divisions that separate conventional political rivals.

How we view the human species constitutes the point of departure for any philosophical or political orientation towards the world. Previous debates about nature and nurture and the human potential still retain their relevance but are subordinate to the far more critical question of whether or not we consider humans as special or unique. Those who do so share a common ground in countering a growing tendency to denigrate the meaning of human.

The downsizing of the role of the subject has as its cultural reinforcement the tendency to denigrate humanity. The construction of a past that continually highlights human selfishness and destruction helps the current project of dispossessing people of any unique or positive qualities. Indeed, there is a widespread conviction that it is the development of human civilization, particularly the advance of science and technology, and the resulting subordination of the natural order to the demands of human society, that is the source of today's problems of environmental destruction and social disintegration.

The perception that it is civilization that bears responsibility for the perils we face today assigns an undistinguished if not low status to the human species. At times this sentiment expresses a sense of loathing for humankind. Such sentiments are expressed by members of Earth First! when they chant 'Four Legs Good! Two Legs Bad!' Indeed people are regularly portrayed as loathsome parasites who threaten the existence of the Earth. Human activity is continually blamed for threatening the survival of the globe. Scare stories about the scale of human destruction are regularly transmitted by the media and promoted by advocacy groups and politicians. For example, it was claimed that human activity has reduced the number of surviving birds and fish species by 35 per cent during the past thirty years.[8] This story, which was circulated by the environmentalist news service *Planet Ark* and picked up by the mainstream media, drew a direct correlation between human action and ecological destruction.

The engagement of human beings with nature is frequently represented as *ecocide*, the heedless and deliberate destruction of the environment. Such a highly charged representation of humanity's attempt to domesticate nature attempts to turn this experience into a process akin to genocide or the Holocaust. The title of Broswimmer's polemic *Ecocide: A Short History of the Mass Extinction of Species* captures this sense of loathing towards the human.[9] Ecocide is also the dominant theme of Jared Diamond's recently published *Collapse: How Societies Choose to Fail or Survive*.[10] According to Diamond, ecocide represents the principal threat to global survival. 'Many people fear that ecocide has now come to overshadow nuclear war and emerging diseases as the threat to global civilisations,' observes Diamond.

The depiction of human activity as itself a threat to the world tends to endow this species with an overwhelmingly negative status. Instead of positive transformation and progress, civilization is portrayed as a history of environmental vandalism. This misanthropic sentiment was clearly expressed by Michael Meacher, the former New Labour Minister for the Environment, when, in 2003, he spoke about how 'we are the virus' infecting the Earth's body. His colleague, Labour MP Tony Banks, echoed this sentiment in a proposed motion to the House of Commons. It stated that 'This House ... believes that humans represent the most obscene, perverted, cruel, uncivilised and lethal species ever to inhabit the planet and looks forward to the day when the inevitable asteroid slams into the Earth and wipes them out thus giving Nature the opportunity to start again.'[11] Of course such intense loathing for people represents but an extreme variant of contemporary anti-humanism. But the denigration of humanity that is associated with the downsizing of subjectivity enjoys a powerful resonance in contemporary culture. This development is evident in the elevation of the natural world and of animals on to a par with – if not into a relation of superiority to – human beings. The insistence on the special qualities and superior attributes of humans is sometimes condemned as speciesist, and the term 'human-centric' used to convey a negative connotation.

Humanizing humanism

It is perverse that twenty-first-century society, which relies so much on human ingenuity and science, also encourages deference to Fate. At a time of widespread disenchantment with the record of humanity's achievements, it is important to restore confidence in the capacity of people to reason and influence the course of events. This is a challenge that confronts everyone – of whatever political, philosophical or religious persuasion – who upholds a human-centred orientation towards the world. This task may appear a modest one compared to the grand visions of the past but in our anti-humanist pre-political era its realization is a precondition for the restoration of a climate hospitable to politics.

The reconstitution of the sense of agency and of historical thinking is the prerequisite for the re-engagement of the public with political life. It requires that we uphold humanity's past achievements, including standards of excellence and civilized forms of behaviour and values. Far from representing a yearning for the good old days, overcoming our alienation from the legacy of human achievement helps us deal with the issues thrown up by change. It is through drawing on the achievements of the past that we can embrace change with enthusiasm.

Promoting a consistent belief in human potential underpins progressive thought. A human-centred view of the world recognizes that people can be destructive and that conflicts of interests can lead to devastating outcomes. However, the negative and sometimes horrific experiences of the past two centuries, up to and including the Holocaust, are the price not of progress, but of the lack of it. Contemporary problems are the result not of applying reason, science and knowledge, but of neglecting them and thwarting the human potential.

The humanist intellectual universe needs to be ambitious but open-ended, prepared to countenance the validity of any idea and ready to yield to new experiences. Such a perspective must engage in the process of *humanizing humanism*. Humanizing humanism requires that failure and mistakes are incorporated into the way we regard progress and the exercise of rationality. If human agency is assigned an important role in the making of history, then factors like culture, subjective perception, conflict, contingency and limited knowledge all play a role in the way we engage with the world. Such influences can confuse, distract and disorient. Nevertheless, they provide some of the important experiences from which we learn how to move forward. In a sense progress happens through these experiences in the exercise of subjectivity. Humanizing humanism requires that we stop treating human development as a foregone conclusion. What we need is a humanism that is not a dogma but a perspective oriented to learning from what humans do.

When the inclination is to wallow in the dark side of humanity, it is worth emphasizing that the legacy of the Enlightenment has provided us with a high standard of moral and ethical responsibility. The twentieth century has witnessed appalling atrocities and relapses into barbarism and genocide. Yet though the scale of degradation experienced in modern society may have been greater than in earlier times, it is only in our era that such events would have been popularly regarded with moral opprobrium. Torture, slavery, the slaughter of defeated enemies – before the modern era such activities were generally considered legitimate and went without question. Autocracy, hierarchy, elitism were considered to be features of a natural order vested with divine authority. It is only with the emergence of modern society, with its concepts of democracy and equality, that the possibility of progress and the improvement of humanity in both a material and moral sense arises.

It is ironic that sentiments of moral revulsion against the evils of modern society are often accompanied by a tendency to repudiate the framework of rationality and purposeful intervention in nature and society that make a more truly human society possible. What we need is a more balanced assessment of the state of society, one that rejects the gross exaggeration of problems and recognizes what we have achieved. But most important of all we need to understand that whatever the mistakes we have made we can extract from them lessons that can guide us to move forward. The reconstitution of agency does not require the invention of grand philosophies but the humanizing of humanism through empowering personhood. This is a problem that we shall revisit in the final chapter.

The last quarter of a century demonstrates that without a robust sense of agency, politics risks losing its meaning. We have also discovered that politics becomes a caricature of itself when it is disassociated from a sense of wider purpose. At a time when politicians are involved in permanent campaigning it is important to remind ourselves that politics is not meant to exist for its own sake but for a higher reason. Without a sense of meaning, politics turns into a series of arbitrary acts that, as we shall see, have a detrimental effect on the workings of public life.

The *modus vivendi* of the cultural and political elites exhibits a startling absence of purpose. They have internalized the mood of political exhaustion and appear as an elite without a focus or a mission. They have no crusade to pursue and no strong convictions about values that give meaning to public life. Consequently, politics presents itself not as the means to accomplish something significant but as an end in itself. Winning elections, scoring points on television interviews or cultivating a network of allies have little rationale other than to reinforce the position and status of individual members of the oligarchy. Periodically, individual members of the elite become aware of the meaninglessness of their activities and demand the restoration of a higher purpose to politics. Hillary Clinton's 'politics of meaning' speech in Austin, Texas in 1993 lamented the feeble role assigned to ideals in American public life. She expressed disquiet about an economy which 'knows the price of everything, but the value of nothing'. As the partner of a president whose election slogan was 'It's the economy, stupid,' the affirmation of a politics of meaning promised a reorientation in a new direction. Unfortunately, speeches upholding morals tend to have a rhetorical character and little practical consequence. 'It is values that sustain communities', declared Tony Blair in his 'politics of meaning' speech at Tübingen University in June 2000. Five years later, the values that inspire his Government's policies are still unclear.

In the aftermath of the victory of George W. Bush in the 2004 US Presidential elections, the call for the introduction of a moral dimension to public life was voiced by numerous commentators. Many Democrats called for the inclusion of 'faith-based politics' in their platform. The reason why this subject reappeared on the agenda had little to do with anything intrinsic to moral concerns. It was a pragmatic turn towards values because it appeared that values could win elections. This message was eloquently spelled out in Thomas Frank's influential *What's The Matter With America?*, which was published in the run-up to the election. 'From the left they hear nothing, but from the Cons they get an explanation for it all,' complained Frank.[1] Frank believes that values are important because they can connect with what he refers to as 'they' – that is, normal people. Across the Atlantic, this point was echoed by Douglas Alexander, the UK's Foreign Office minister, in his pamphlet *Telling It Like It Could Be*. Alexander argues that without a moral impulse his Labour Party will fail to inspire the electorate and even demoralize its supporters.[2]

There is something of an air of desperation among Democrats as they hunt for some moral values they can buy into. Jim Wallis' *God's Politics: Why the Right Gets It Wrong and the Left Doesn't Get It* became an instant bestseller as Democrats looked for ready-made moral formulae with which they could connect with ordinary folk.[3] Wallis, billed as a left-wing Evangelical, is critical of 'secular fundamentalists' and offers moral values to the disoriented liberal. The problem with politically motivated calls for the restoration of a moral dimension to public life is that they are driven by the instrumental purpose of gaining or retaining power. However, a morality that is manufactured in response to the demands of political pragmatism lacks an organic relationship to lived experience and is therefore unlikely to find resonance amongst the wider public. And an unfocused and disconnected oligarchy is unlikely to possess sufficient sensitivity to the day-to-day problems confronting human beings to engage with the existential issues facing society. That is why the pragmatic search for a ready-made moral purpose usually turns into an arbitrary exercise of picking and choosing some inoffensive values. Alexander ends up by opting for the public service ethos of the National Health Service and tackling world poverty. But it could as easily have been world peace or compassion towards the infirm. Such arbitrary lists of values simply serve as a testimony to the absence of a purposeful moral perspective that is organic to contemporary public life.

Of course individual public figures like Alexander are genuine in their search for a higher purpose. But what they often overlook is that the problem of political exhaustion cannot be tackled by clever people attending a brainstorming session at a seminar. Nor is the problem simply that of morality in the abstract. As indicated previously, the restoration of genuine public life involves rethinking the meaning of what it means to be human. An authentic grammar of morality is always embedded in a clear conception of what it means to be human. Promoting a culture that valorizes people's potential and agency represents the point of departure for any agenda that attempts to endow politics with a sense of purpose. Unfortunately, this is an orientation that today's political class is unlikely to adopt. Why? Because it not only lacks faith in human nature but, as we shall see, also exhibits contempt for ordinary folk.

Contempt for the public

The political elite's concern with morality is often motivated
by the apprehension that unless it is able to engage with the big
questions faced by ordinary folk, it will lose all points of
contact with the public. It also fears that unless it can project
some positive values onto society, people will become
influenced by value-driven extremist religious and political
movements that are hostile to the status quo. This sentiment is
underpinned by the patronizing assumption that, unlike the
elite, ordinary people need simple answers about the meaning
of life. It is not the elite who need moral direction but ordinary
people who will otherwise fall prey to the siren call of
extremists. This sentiment is particularly pronounced amongst
sections of the cultural elite who, in private conversation,
regard ordinary people – 'rednecks', Nascar dads, soccer
mums, tabloid readers and so forth – as far too crass,
materialistic, simplistic, racist, sexist, homophobic and emotionally illiterate. The elite favourably contrast their adherence
to diversity and multiculturalism to the 'fundamentalism' and
intolerance of a simple-minded public.

Blaming the appeal of fundamentalism – for example, the
demand for moral values – on the receptivity of ordinary folk to
simplistic black-and-white solutions tends to shift focus from the
failure of the elite to promote and uphold a positive vision of the
future to the alleged political illiteracy of the people. Discussion
of so-called fundamentalist movements like the US-based
Christian Right often contains an implicit condemnation of the
people that support them. They are castigated for lacking the
sophistication required to engage with the 'uncertainties' thrown
up by a 'complex' and 'fluid' world. According to Frank,
American people are so thick that they don't even know what's in
their best interest. 'People getting their fundamental interests
wrong is what American political life is all about,' he notes.[4] The

cultural elite often flatters itself for not being like them since it is freed of the burden of any fundamental principles.

The term 'cosmopolitanism' has been used to describe attitudes associated with an elite that has freed itself from tradition-based moral or ideological baggage. Cosmopolitanism is favourably contrasted with the widely used bogey term 'fundamentalism', which refers to individuals and communities who possess strong beliefs. To take an illustration of this approach:

> While reactionary groups struggle to hold the line, often by trying to impose threatened moral values on the rest of society, those who are more adaptive to the transformation of society often engage in remarkable explorations of self and identity, forming new types of families, new spiritual movements, exchanging world art and music, exploring new jobs and careers, attributing less importance to nation and government, and forming cosmopolitan ties with others in distant parts of the world.[5]

The fluid and open-ended character of cosmopolitan ties leading to the 'remarkable explorations of self and identity' serves as the model to adopt against those who are determined to 'impose threatened moral values on the rest of society'. But the cosmopolitan elite is far from confident about its ability to find resonance for its fluid values in the rest of society. That is why it periodically needs to demonstrate that it, too, can convey a sense of moral purpose.

After the re-election of George W. Bush, many Democrats and supporters of New Labour drew the conclusion that the reason why the Republicans succeeded was because they had a simple moral message that appealed to the fundamentalist sensibilities of people. 'The republican campaign was about reaching out to people and asking them to affirm their shared moral values,' writes Alexander, before adding the clincher that the 'people responded so that the Republicans won'.[6] It was suggested that the Democrats were too 'intellectual' and too 'rational' to make headway with many politically illiterate voters. The conclusion drawn was that an appeal to moral concerns could resonate with popular emotion in a way that reasoned arguments could not. The implication of this argument is that rational and intellectual arguments are likely to have little purchase on an otherwise simple-minded electorate. In the past, conservatives used to argue that the people need religion so that they can know their place in society. Today it is sections of the so-called left who want to inject the public with a dose of moral direction. In both cases, morality is specifically for the masses. This cynical orientation towards the public was clearly spelled out by William Davies of the London-based Institute for Public Policy Research. 'The liberal, secular left has somehow to find ways of supplying citizens with emotional and metaphysical comforts even when it does not itself believe in such things,' he warned.[7] This provision of so-called metaphysical comforts serves the same function that adult-invented cautionary tales play for children.

Instead of acknowledging the absence of any higher purpose for its brand of cosmopolitan outlook, the cultural elite prefers to indict ordinary folk for being simple and gullible. In the US, this paternalistic impulse led some Democratic Party activists to blame their electoral defeats on the stupidity of the people. One liberal activist, Michael Gronewalter, notes that 'civility and intelligent dialogue are useful tools among intelligent people', but are inappropriate for engaging with the wider public. He argues that the problem is that 'we as liberals are in general far more intelligent, well reasoned and educated and will go to astonishingly great lengths to convince people of the integrity and validity of our fair and well-thought-out arguments', but the audience is not paying attention and *'isn't always getting it'*.[8] This point was reinforced by Arianna Huffington. 'Thanks to the Bush campaign's unremitting fear-mongering, millions of voters are reacting not with their linear and logical left brain but with their lizard brain and their more emotional right brain,' she observed.[9]

Casual throwaway remarks about the stupidity of the American public by media commentators often convey a profound sense of contempt towards one's moral inferior. One columnist in *The Village Voice* writes of the 'monumental apathy and programmed ignorance of at least half the American public'.[10] 'Do you feel like you live in a nation of idiots?' asks the consummate cynic, Michael Moore, before adding 'I used to console myself about the state of stupidity in this country by repeating to myself: *Even if there are two hundred million stone-cold idiots in this country, that leaves at least eighty million who'll get what I am saying – and that's still more than the population of the United Kingdom and Ireland combined!'*[11]

American cynics do not have a monopoly on a sense of loathing for common people. '*HOW CAN 59 MILLION PEOPLE BE SO DUMB?*' was the headline of the British tabloid the *Daily Mirror* the day after the 2004 US Presidential election. As far as this paper was concerned, the 59,054,087 people who voted for George Bush were just plain stupid. The view that the public is too moronic to grasp the high-minded and complex ideals of a very sophisticated cosmopolitan elite expresses a profound sense of contempt for human beings. This disparagement of people also serves as a form of self-flattery for an elite that otherwise has little to shout about. By uncritically transferring responsibility for the contemporary malaise of political life on the back of an uneducated electorate, it distracts attention from its own sense of moral confusion.

Disconnected elite

Pointing the finger of blame for the political malaise at the public is at best an act of self-deception by an elite that lacks belief in its own institution and authority. As Bauman notes, 'unlike their ancestors of the nation-building era, global elites have no mission to perform: they do not feel the need or intend to proselytize, to carry the torch of wisdom, to enlighten, instruct and convert'.[12] Their promotion of the ideal of diversity and multiculturalism is represented as a statement of tolerance. But a celebration of diversity can also represent an attempt to evade the need to take a stand on any specific value that transcends the plurality of different sentiments. At best, diversity describes the multiplicity of human experience. Diversity is a term of description and not a value or a moral category. The fraudulent project of treating diversity as an end in itself serves as an escape clause for an elite that lacks the capacity to believe in a clearly formulated moral purpose.

This absence of a moral purpose coexists with a sense of cynicism towards society's institutions. Today's elite lacks a *l'espirit de corps* or the capacity to assume responsibility for the institutions that support its authority. As Dalton notes in his study of political attitudes, surveys indicate that the 'current malaise of the political process is born amongst those who will sustain and lead the system'.[13] The weak attachment of today's elite towards its own institutions is not the product of a failure of individual character. Rather, this estrangement from the source of its authority is influenced by the difficulty it has in endowing its position with legitimacy. The process of political exhaustion is experienced by today's elite as a crisis of legitimacy. This concern is refracted through interminable discussions about the problem of trust, the issue of accountability. The obsession with governance and the process of governing, rather than with its purpose, is symptomatic of the aspiration to construct institutional arrangements that are perceived as legitimate by a wider public.

Today's problem of legitimacy has little to do with the phenomenon of a classical crisis of legitimacy. Unlike the latter, which in part is provoked by a systematic challenge to the prevailing authority from below, today's problem is mainly the result of a process of disintegration within the elite itself. This process of disintegration is, to a point at least, a symptom of the state of political exhaustion in which society finds itself. Moreover, in the absence of any alternative or serious challenge, today's elite is under little pressure to close ranks. As a result, its problem of legitimacy is experienced as a process of internally driven implosion or the gradual unravelling of its authority. The loss of legitimacy is not associated with any specific political threat. Indeed, if it faced such a threat, today's elite might even regain a semblance of coherence or self-definition. The problem of legitimacy is experienced through the feeling of being disconnected and detached from the rest of society. The sensation of being out of touch is a dominant theme in the deliberation of the political classes. Opinion polls, deliberative polling, focus groups, citizens' juries and a thousand other varieties of consultation exercises represent a desperate attempt to put an otherwise disconnected elite in touch with popular opinion.

Public life today is dominated by a series of futile initiatives designed to assist the political class in overcoming its isolation from the wider world. As I noted in an earlier study, *Where Have All the Intellectuals Gone?*, politicians are 'drawn towards new infantalizing initiatives designed to "reconnect" with the public'.[14] As a result, there is a perceptible tendency to reinterpret democratic participation as a diffuse notion of 'having your say'. As we shall see, considerable energy is devoted to the construction of a project that attempts to bypass the problem of public engagement by degrading the meaning of democracy. Under the guise of democratizing public life, a new oligarchy devoted to an elite-driven brand of pseudo-participation has emerged.

The politics of the lobbyist-activist

Outwardly it appears that the political class is driven by an unprecedented commitment to democratize society. It is continually reforming institutions and proposing to make old ones more transparent and accountable. Governments love consulting the people, and so-called stakeholders and advocacy groups are frequently asked to front initiatives. In Europe in particular, politicians are often enthusiastic about ceding some of their power to new more 'enlightened' institutions based in Brussels. There is even the beginning of a new ideology of cosmopolitanism that promises to extend democracy by freeing it of its national constraint.

Anyone inspired by a humanist vision of the world is naturally supportive of measures that encourage global cooperation and harmony. In principle, the tendency to transcend the confines of the nation state to realize a more global objective should be welcomed. However, the current trend towards the construction of a 'global civil society' is characteristically motivated by a profoundly anti-democratic impulse. It is encouraged by a political class that feels exposed and estranged from its own national institutions. The turn towards cosmopolitanism is in part triggered by the desire to avoid taking responsibility for the consequences of its actions.

At least in its present form, cosmopolitan democracy is a contradiction in terms. Whatever the limits of parliamentary democracy, people at least enjoy the formal right of electing representatives and holding them to account. If nothing else, people are in a position to put pressure on institutions that are embedded within their own region or territory. And in exceptional circumstances, if their representatives prove inflexible and unresponsive, the public can directly respond, protesting, rebelling or even getting rid of them. Whatever the defects of national institutions, the problems of genuine participation are likely to be far greater in the case of international ones. At least in this respect, advocates of a global civil society adopt the double standard of criticizing the democratic deficit of national institutions while avoiding tackling a far greater tendency towards international bureaucratization. As one critic of this double standard notes, proponents of global civil society 'assume that transnational organizations can assist world-wide democratization without questioning either the representativeness of such organisations or their accountability'.[15]

Advocates of cosmopolitan democracy promote a vague incoherent doctrine that has little to say about genuine public engagement. According to one account, 'democracy should be seen as an *endless* process, such that we lack the ability to predict today the direction in which future generations will push the forms of contestation, participation and management'.[16] This emphasis on process rather than the substance of democracy reflects a cavalier attitude towards the notion of representation. This attitude is not surprising since cosmopolitan consciousness is bitterly hostile to the ideal of sovereignty, which it regards as a 'dogma to overcome'.[17] Hostility to sovereignty and support for 'political denationalization' is inspired by the objective of insulating politics from public pressure. That is why cosmopolitanism is bitterly hostile to what it characterizes as populism, which it considers to be the 'Achilles' heel of International Institutions'.[18] Populism is used by its detractors as a term to describe people and movements who have failed to internalize the views deemed correct by the political elite. One supporter of cosmopolitanism is 'worried about the resistance of societies and not the nation state to international institutions'.[19] In other words, the problem confronting cosmopolitanism is not the political class that manage the institutions of the nation state but the 'resistance of societies', that is of 'ordinary people'. According to this interpretation, an enlightened network of cosmopolitan elites needs to contain 'broad national societal coalitions' that are hostile to their project.

Cosmopolitanism puts its faith not in the people but in civil society, which actually means a network of pressure groups and non-governmental organizations (NGOs). According to the cosmopolitan worldview, NGOs and lobby groups constitute the vanguard of an enlightened society. These organizations, which are also often called new social movements, are assigned the project of democratizing 'everyday life'. Paradoxically, the advocacy of new social movements is justified on the ground that representative democracy has failed to engage the public. It is argued that social movements have provided people with the means for participating in activities that really matter to them. In contradistinction to parliamentary democracy, protest movements are presented as providing an opportunity for genuine participatory democracy. They claim that 'those who advocate the merits of participatory democracy' expect 'the involvement of the electorate to be beyond voting'.[20]

Supporters of new social movements frequently counterpose voter apathy with the activism of protest movements. 'Whilst the movement has gone from strength to strength, voter apathy has increased, and voter turnout has fallen to record lows', argues one proponent.[21] The possibility that the impact of these movements depends on the perpetuation of public disengagement is not considered by supporters of the politics of lobbying. Yet there is considerable evidence that NGOs and social movements have adopted a highly elitist style of activism. In an important study titled *Diminishing Democracy*, Theda Skocpol argues that American advocacy groups and NGOs rarely seek to engage ordinary people. Instead they are involved in a form of 'top-down communication'. They rely less on mobilizing grass-roots opinion than on influencing opinion makers.[22] Indeed, it can be argued that advocacy groups and many protest movements are an integral part of the oligarchical network constructed by the political class. That is why protest movements – particularly consumer and environmentalist activism – enjoy an almost unprecedented degree of adulation in the media and public life.

Non-profit institutions often brag of their independence from the market and government, but actually 'they are profoundly intertwined with both, especially with government', concludes Skocpol.[23] They are frequently financed by foundations, companies and public bodies. Skocpol's study indicates that they are far less likely to be membership-based than in the past. They are professional institutions that are in the business of 'Doing-For' instead of 'Doing-With' people. As well as being 'staff-heavy and focused on lobbying, research, and media projects', 'they are managed from the top, even when they claim to speak for ordinary people'.[24] Unlike traditional social movements, organizations that brand themselves as civil society groups are essentially lobbying groups, uninterested in mobilizing popular support *per se*. They are predominantly media-focused organizations whose main objective is gaining publicity. The significance which advocacy groups, NGOs and campaigning groups attach to publicity is motivated by the realization that their influence is intimately linked to their public profile. Indeed, their influence over society is dependent on how successfully they raise their public profile. Consequently, the machinery of civil-society activism is single-mindedly oriented towards gaining publicity through the media. A large active membership is quite unnecessary for an organization commited to oiling the network of the political oligarchy. Contacts in the media and friends in influential places are far more important than thousands of active supporters. Even when the new social movement activists take direct action, what counts is the presence of the television camera. There is little point in protesting or demonstrating if it does not gain publicity for the group concerned. From this perspective, an act is deemed effective if it makes the news. The typical Greenpeace stunt involving a small core of professional protestors, whose appearance is carefully crafted for the maximum dramatic effect, is emblematic of the political theatre of new social movement activism.

For its part, the media enjoys and even embraces the civil-society activist. For example, in the UK, campaigns against road building, live-animal exports, the fast food chain McDonald's and trials of genetically modified foods are characteristically portrayed as acts of responsible citizenship. In recent times, the media depicted environmentalists who wrecked GM crop test sites as people's Davids tackling giant American Goliaths. According to John Vidal, the environmental editor of the *Guardian*, 'the ecological-inspired critique of democracy is now exploding and the crop pullers should be seen as part of an international movement that, thanks to email and the web, watchdog groups and increasing networking, is throwing up new issues, philosophies, ethics, and legal arguments'.[25]

This representation of environmental activists as innovators who are providing a morally exhausted society with philosophical contributions is rarely interrogated. At every turn, semi-official activists are praised for their altruism, social responsibility and moral outlook. Campaigns such as 'Make Poverty History' have the status of semi-official projects.

The adoption of the cause of new social movement activism by sections of the current British political establishment raises interesting questions about its status. Consumer and environmental activists routinely attempt to portray themselves as disadvantaged radical outsiders who are continually battling against powerful vested interests. Environmental activists, in particular, claim that they represent a disenfranchised public who lack any significant access to the political system. However, judging by the highly positive representation of these 'outsiders' by the mainstream media, one could be forgiven for drawing the conclusion that such activism is very much led by 'insiders'.

As we noted in our discussion of 'Politics in Denial', proponents of pressure-group activism go so far as to refute the idea that society is afflicted by the scourge of apathy and social engagement. The success of protest groups in gaining media profile is interpreted as a positive reorientation of the public from the irrelevance of formal politics to more meaningful forms of engagement. Some analysts even go so far as to present people's involvement in single-issue lobbying as proof of young people's yearning for genuine participation. Cherny claims that young people have rejected the old bureaucratic structures of party politics in favour of genuine participation through activism.[26] This tendency to invest voluntary associations with a progressive mission overlooks one crucial problem, which is that these groups engage far fewer individuals than even the existing discredited political institutions. While the emergence of local civic organizations can play a useful role in contributing to the development of a society's political culture, it is unlikely that they can compensate for the effects of the public's disengagement from national political life. As Skocpol concludes: 'professionally managed, top-down civic endeavours simultaneously limit the mobilization of most citizens into public life and encourage a fragmentation of social identities and trivial polarizations in public debates'.

Protest has not only become highly respectable, it has also secured a semi-official mandate to break the law. Anti-GM food protesters are often represented as idealist young people who are acting on our behalf. As part of the British political oligarchy, they have the kind of freedom to protest that is usually denied to ordinary mortals. When Lord Meltchett, the aristocratic former leader of Greenpeace, was arrested for criminal damage and theft, he was genuinely shocked by his treatment. As far as he was concerned, his action was a 'direct expression of "people's power" '. As the self-appointed voice of the British people, Greenpeace feels entitled to undertake any form of direct action that it deems necessary to keep 'democracy healthy and responsive'.

Meltchett, like many other leading lobbyists, has an elitist notion of democracy. It is driven by the conviction that if one believes that something is wrong, then waiting for an unresponsive political system to do something about it is a luxury that society cannot afford. Professional environmental protesters assume that they have the moral authority to take matters into their own hands since they are acting on behalf of the People. They believe that their unique philosophical insights entitle them to act in the best way they think fit.

One of the key arguments used by consumer activists to justify their mandate to break the law is that the political system is not really democratic, and is unresponsive to the demands of ordinary people. Doug Parr, the campaigns director of Greenpeace UK, argues that the public have made their views on GM foods absolutely clear and that his organization is merely acting on the expressed will of the people. But how does Parr know that Greenpeace has a democratic warrant to break the law? It appears that people's fears about GM food 'come up time and again in focus groups'. For Parr, the focus group, a traditional instrument of market research, represents an arena for the expression of the popular will. Another barometer used by the campaign director of Greenpeace to gauge the will of the people is their shopping habits. 'When Greenpeace "decontaminated" a farm-scale trial, it was acting on behalf of people whose views were not being represented,' writes Parr. Why? Because 'the public had already demonstrated its views very strongly by forcing GM foods off the supermarket shelves'. Consumer suspicion towards GM foods is represented as an act akin to casting a vote in a ballot box. According to this logic, if people become averse to cornflakes and succeed in forcing it off the shelves of supermarkets, they would also have the moral authority to wreck the plant producing this stigmatized commodity.

Parr also claims that protestors have acted on behalf of people whose views are otherwise not represented. How does he know? From focus groups? From market research into people's shopping habits? For a self-appointed representative of the public, the conviction of righteousness is sufficient to justify action. It appears that the cosmopolitan critique of parliamentary democracy is driven by the motive of providing protesters with a carte-blanche to break the law. George Monbiot, a prominent journalist and environmental campaigner, contends that disruptive protest is a civic duty. Why? Because 'Parliament is incompletely representative ... It tends to concentrate on the concerns of target voters and powerful institutions, rather than those of the poor, the vulnerable or the unborn,' writes Monbiot.[27] By dragging in even the unborn, Monbiot is able to construct a formidable constituency whose voice is ignored by Parliament. In turn, the claim to be able to speak on behalf of people not yet born suggests the kind of supernatural powers that ordinary politicians manifestly lack.

There is little doubt that parliamentary democracy is imperfect and generally subject to vested interest. Most people have little say over the way that society is conducted, and the political oligarchy possesses interests which often contradict what is good for society. Nevertheless, people at least have a formal right to elect people to speak on their behalf. Whatever the defects of parliamentary democracy, it at least invites people to vote for individuals and parties that reflect their preference. This political system also allows people – albeit infrequently – to get rid of politicians who have lost the support of the electorate. Paradoxically, this system of defective democracy is far superior to the so-called active citizenship of civil society groups. Why? An elected politician and party at least has a mandate to speak on behalf of the public. In contrast, Lord Meltchett can only speak for his colleagues who gave him his post at the Soil Association. The issue is not whether Meltchett is right or wrong about a particular subject, but that he is entitled to speak only for himself and no one else. Lord Meltchett can no more claim to speak on my behalf than can the director of any voluntary association. In contrast, my MP – with whom I largely disagree – has at least the right to claim to be my representative.

In reality, the lobbyist-activist critique of representative democracy is fundamentally an anti-democratic one. It is based on the premise that unelected individuals who possess a lofty moral purpose have a greater right to act on the public's behalf than politicians elected through an imperfect political process. Environmentalist campaigners, who derive their mandate from a self-selected network of advocacy groups, represent a far narrower constituency than an elected politician. Judging by their record, the response of advocacy groups to the genuine problem of democratic accountability is to avoid it altogether, opting instead for interest-group lobbying.

The professionalization of protest suggests that a significant section of social movements have been absorbed into the institutions of the political oligarchy. This development is most strikingly evident during the high-profile international summits that provide the focus for much cosmopolitan protest these days. At these summits there is a place for everyone. The conventional politicians and their officials meet to decide the 'future of the world'. In the meantime, they are lobbied by legions of NGOs, who hold slightly less conventional meetings in 'alternative sites'. And on the streets are the angry protestors, who have flown from all over the world to air the views of people whose voices would not otherwise be heard. Cosmopolitan democracy in action turns into a carnival of networking, lobbying, working the media and obligatory protest performances on the street. This network is part of a public world that is far more oligarchical than in the past. As Skocpol notes, 'early twenty-first-century Americans live in a diminished democracy, in a much less participatory and more oligarchicly managed civic world'.[28]

There is an important critique to be made about the formal and incomplete character of representative democracy. But the advocates of cosmopolitanism and new social movements are motivated less by a passion for democracy than the desire to gain a semblance of connection with people. That is why activism, even when conducted by small groups of professional lobbyists, is often treated as another hopeful sign of democratic revival.

Bypassing democracy

Critics of representative democracy are rarely committed to tackling the issues thrown up by the social disengagement of the public. On the contrary, the activism of a small minority of lobbyists serves as a pragmatic alternative to public engagement. Instead of seeking to revitalize the democratic ethos, the ideologues of civil society promote exercises in consultation. They advocate the idea of deliberative democracy as an enlightened alternative to representative democracy. Deliberative democracy usually means a small forum where people can engage in face-to-face conversation and allegedly have time to reason with one another.

It is argued that deliberative democracy provides participation with meaning since participants are involved in a dialogue that directly leads to a discernible outcome. Just what consequences these decisions have is rarely discussed. This is not surprising since deliberative democrats believe that deliberation is an end in itself. This focus on consultation displaces the meaning of democracy as an instrument for involving the public in the running of society, in favour of the technique of formal consultation. As Gorg and Hirsch argue, this orientation serves to 'render the concept of democracy redundant', as it turns it into a 'purely consultation process'.[29]

In reality, consultation turns into a tool of management that masquerades as genuine deliberation. The initiative for deliberation always comes from above, and the terms on which the exercise is enacted are constructed by professional consultants.

The process of deliberation depends on 'procedures, techniques and methods' worked out by experts.[30] The procedure itself is administered by professional facilitators whose rules are designed to assist the management of participants. This is not a forum where the participants interact as equals. Skilled facilitators are employed to create the right kind of environment and the desirable outcomes. A discussant of the virtues of 'citizens' juries' notes that they rely on 'trained moderators' who ensure 'fair proceedings'.[31] Yet without a hint of self-consciousness this highly manipulative environment is endorsed as a superior alternative to 'liberal institutions' which encourage the passivity of citizens.[32] What we have is the pretence of deliberation and the reality of manipulation.

Nor are deliberative democrats reluctant to acknowledge the fact that their support for such forums is contingent on the participants arriving at the right kinds of decisions. Deliberative democracy is often supported on the ground that it provides an environment conducive for people to change their minds and adopt the ethos favoured by the forum's organizers. Deliberation is favoured because it can act as a vehicle for transmitting the outlook of the organizers. To ensure that this objective is realized, the groups' interpersonal dynamic is carefully controlled. To prevent the spontaneous emergence of informal group leaders, 'most moderators are alert to the manner in which deliberations can be dominated by confident and outspoken individuals', argues a contribution on the subject.[33] It appears that deliberative democracy works best when 'confident and outspoken individuals' are put in their place.

Some advocates of deliberative democracy regard it as a form of social engineering through which the participants can be manipulated to arrive at the 'correct' outcome. Hoggett and Thompson look upon deliberative democracy as a vehicle for the emotional management of the participants. They fear that if a group is allowed the freedom to develop its own emotional dynamic, the wrong decisions may be made. 'In extreme circumstances, we may judge that a group came to the wrong conclusion since its collective emotions had too strong an influence on its deliberations,' they note. There is little scope here for genuine political debate and dialogue. People can deliberate as long as they arrive at the 'right conclusion'. To realize this objective, Hoggett and Thompson advise the adoption of 'technologies of deliberation', such as 'the use of moderators and facilitators, small break-out groups, warm-up sessions and other methods for maximizing the effectiveness of juries' deliberations'.[34] It is a sign of the times that a procedure that could come straight from Orwell's *Nineteen Eighty-Four* can be represented as an enlightened alternative to representative democracy. The assumption that the professional facilitator has the moral authority to determine how people should feel is symptomatic of a patronizing orientation towards the 'deliberators'.

In former times, social engineering was directed towards a clearly formulated objective, such as using education to achieve a more egalitarian society. Today, initiatives like the management of people's emotions are not connected to a wider political agenda. Such schemes have no purpose other than allowing the disconnected elites to establish new points of contact with the public. Connecting, interacting and participating are depicted as possessing positive virtues in their own right. That is why *social inclusion* has emerged as the principal virtue celebrated by the cultural and political elite.

The experience of disconnection has enhanced the sensitivity of the political elites to the problem of social cohesion. This problem is not unique to our times. Since the early nineteenth century, modern societies have periodically experienced a crisis of values. In the past, conservatives, liberal, radicals and even social democrats recognized that without a consensus built on a common web of meaning society becomes disoriented and confused. Left-wingers and conservatives disagreed only about the forms through which a sense of moral purpose could be achieved. Whereas right-wingers proposed the revival of old-style Christianity, radicals considered that traditional religion had been discredited or had become irrelevant to modern times. They advocated new secular faiths, often closely linked to science, as an alternative.

The situation today is very different to past attempts to find a sense of moral purpose. Today's elite have adopted the more modest mission of turning their own aspiration for reconnection into a moral value. Participation *per se* is invested with moral meaning. It is frequently presented as an end in itself. Inclusion or social inclusion is the principal moral virtue in the current political vocabulary. The term 'social inclusion' is frequently used in a rhetorical or diffuse manner. Whilst it lacks any precise meaning it expresses the distinct orientation that the political classes have towards the public. Inclusion is essentially about institutionalizing participation and involvement in as many settings as possible. As is the case with the focus groups initiated by deliberative democrats, 'inclusive institutions' need not have any power or influence over issues that matter to people. Inclusion is its own virtue – it matters little what one is included in. The political agenda of inclusion is usually associated with the diffuse notion of 'having your say'. A model inclusive institution is one where everyone's voice can be heard and where everyone can feel that he or she has had their say. Having a say has little to do with the ability to exercise influence or possess power. It amounts to little more than the therapeutic exercise of letting off steam. This pretence of participation serves as the model for aiding the political class to 'reconnect' with an otherwise distant public.

The elite has whole-heartedly adopted the project of giving people a 'voice', especially those deemed to be excluded. In practice, this means creating venues for inclusion. Take the following list of venues designed to 'include diverse actors in deliberative processes' – 'citizens' juries, citizens' panels, committees, consensus conferences, scenario workshops, deliberative polling, focus groups, multi-criteria mapping, public meetings, rapid and participatory rural appraisal and visioning exercises'.[35] What characterizes all these institutions is that they have no purpose other than to establish a point of contact between the included and their disconnected elite.

The imperative of inclusion has also impacted on existing institutions. Schools, universities, museums, libraries, sport and community organizations, and theatres are just some of the institutions whose purpose has been reconfigured around the task of inclusion. The pressure to include has forced many of these institutions to lose sight of what was the original purpose of their existence. Anything that prevents inclusion – high standards, rigorous expectations, challenging encounters, demanding engagements – has to give way to it. Not surprisingly, flattering the public has become part of the ethos of cultural and educational institutions. For the elite, the dumbing down of culture appears a small price to pay for the opportunity to connect with the public.

The main consequence of the promotion of inclusion is to compound the problem of political exhaustion by rendering public life banal. Intelligent people rarely want to be given a voice by distant bureaucratic institutions – they want to be taken seriously. At best, such top-down initiatives are experienced as a form of largesse or entitlement. Sadly, in some cases this encourages people to acquire a sense of *unearned* entitlement. Flattery can create a demand for more flattery, the institutionalization of which tragically serves to distract people from confronting the challenge facing them.

Nor does social engineering have the desired result of reconnecting the political class with the people. After more than two decades of policies promoting inclusion, the political class is more and not less isolated from the people. The dumbing down of public life in fact limits opportunities for the genuine exchange of experience and exploration of new ideas. Yet developing new ideas is critical for tackling the current state of political malaise. The future of democracy depends on engagement with issues of substance.

Social inclusion is frequently presented as an important dimension in the democratization of life. Inclusive institutions are meant to be more democratic than exclusive ones because everyone is welcome in them. 'In complex societies, democracy consists in enabling individuals and groups to affirm themselves and to be recognised for what they are or what they wish to be,' argues one advocate of inclusion.[36] However, this equation of democracy with being granted a voice represents a fundamental redefinition of this important political concept. Real democracy is not the gift of affirmation bestowed on the people. It is a form of political life that provides opportunities for people to participate in and influence the decisions that affect their lives. The institutionalization of inclusion seeks to bypass the problem of democracy. It also bypasses the question of meaning. It offers inclusion and the opportunity to 'have your say' as a substitute for a politics of purpose. Involvement becomes an end in itself and the task of confronting the purpose of politics is avoided.

7   The Politics of Fear

The absence of political purpose and clarity about the future continually encourages the cultural sensibility that we describe as the conservatism of fear. In public life this sensibility is often experienced as the *politics of fear*. In recent years it has become common for one group of politicians to denounce their opponents for practising such politics.

The term 'politics of fear' contains the implication that politicians self-consciously manipulate people's anxieties in order to realize their objectives. There is little doubt that they do regard fear as an important resource for gaining a hearing for their message. Scare tactics can sometimes work to undermine opponents and to gain the acquiescence of the electorate. However, as we shall see, the politics of fear is not simply about the manipulation of public opinion. It exists as a force in its own right. Nevertheless, political elites, public figures, sections of the media and campaigners are directly culpable for using fear to promote their agenda.

Commentaries on the politics of fear tend to treat the phenomenon as an isolated trend, and therefore overlook the fact that it is the inevitable consequence of the prevailing mood of political exhaustion. A fatalisitic sensibility coexists with anxieties concerning the future, which in turn disposes the public to feel uncomfortable about managing uncertainty. The image of 'letting the genie out of the bottle' to signal disquiet is, for example, frequently used when news breaks of a potentially exciting innovation. In such circumstances, even professional politicians who are in the business of promoting fear are themselves habitually overwhelmed by it. As noted in the previous chapter, a disconnected elite lacks cohesion and a sense of purpose. Confronted with its inner confusion it often conveys a sense of disorientation and defensiveness. And, from time to time, its own inner anxieties are articulated in public through the idiom of fear. The politics of fear is rightly seen as a manipulative project that aims to immobilize public dissent. It *is* that, but it is also the mantra with which a disconnected elite readily responds in the circumstances of its isolation. As we shall see, one of the attractions of the politics of fear is that it absolves its practitioners from having to formulate what it actually stands for.

As a currency of public discourse

The emergence of the current discussion on the politics of fear has been stimulated by the belief that it has become one of the defining features of public life in the post-9/11 era. Most commentators associate it with the style of governance practised by the Bush administration, and many attribute Bush's re-election to the impact such politics have had on the American electorate. The main charge made against Bush is that fear has become his favourite weapon of choice, and that since 9/11 the public's fear of terrorism has been systematically manipulated to strengthen his Government's authority. Many of the subsequent curbs on civil rights, such as the post-9/11 Patriot Act, are represented as symptoms of a trend towards the exercise of domination through fear. 'Since 9/11 the politics of fear has become the point of intersection between the political/corporate elites who run this country' and 'it has been a great strength of the Bush administration', writes an academic critic.[1] For some observers the very fact that Bush won the November 2004 election is itself a testimony to the formidable power of the politics of fear: 'it is increasingly apparent that the climate of fear promoted by the Bush Administration in the wake of a series of national traumas is having a wide effect', warns the editor of the online publication *AlterNet*.[2] Since the 2004 election, opponents routinely portray virtually every Bush initiative as an example of such politics. So, in January 2005, the Democratic Senator Edward Kennedy argued that Bush's policy on Social Security was pushed through using the politics of fear.

In Britain, the Blair Government is frequently the target of similar accusations, just such a charge being levelled against it, for example, when it introduced a series of law-and-order bills to Parliament in November 2004. The then Home Secretary David Blunkett responded that 'this is not about the politics of fear, but about taking sensible and commonsense measures to protect people'.[3] Though many New Labour supporters accept the content of the charge in general, they argue that if they did not pursue it others would. Commenting on Blunkett's bills, one leading supporter of the Government was reported to have said that 'if Labour did not do the politics of fear, it would have the politics of fear done to it'.[4]

During the months leading up to the 2005 British General Election campaign, commentators adopted the politics of fear as a frame through which they interpreted the event. 'The politics of fear is stalking the land,' noted Tony Travers, a political scientist at the London School of Economics. This point was echoed by Oxford academic Guy Goodwin-Gill, who claimed that 'politicians believe that fear and anxiety is the way to win votes'.[5] A few days before the announcement of the Election, Dr Rowan Williams, the Archbishop of Canterbury, published an open letter in which he demanded that all parties should stop pushing fear-driven politics. 'Despite the best intentions, election campaigns can quickly turn into a competition about who can most effectively frighten voters,' argued the Archbishop.[6] Throughout the Election, candidates accused one another of playing the fear card, the close association of politics and fear, by this time, having become an indisputable fact.

Commentators concerned about the politics of fear have tended to identify the war against terrorism as the engine of its growth. That the fear of terrorism can provoke powerful anxieties is an uncontroversial proposition. But it is important to recall that the politicization of the fear of terrorism is not a new development. Even before 9/11, governments could not resist the temptation to play the terror card. Speculation about 'catastrophic terrorism' and 'weapons of mass destruction' was rife in the 1990s. It was President Bill Clinton who appointed a national coordinator for security, infrastructure protection and counter-terrorism in May 1998, in order to 'bring the full force of all of our resources to bear swiftly and effectively'. In November 1998, a group of foreign policy experts claimed that, 'The danger of weapons of mass destruction being used against America and its allies is greater now than at any time since the Cuban missile crisis of 1962.'[7]

By the late 1990s the promotion of fears about catastrophic terrorism was embraced by a variety of political and special interest groups. A few weeks before 9/11, Sir William Stewart, the UK's former chief scientific adviser, warned that the New Labour Government's difficulty in dealing with the foot-and-mouth outbreak showed just how vulnerable Britain was to any future threat from biological warfare.[8] The ease with which he could jump from a crisis of British farming to the spectre of biological warfare highlighted the salience of fear as a political resource today.

Since 9/11, politicians, business, advocacy organizations and special interest groups have sought to further their narrow agendas by manipulating public anxiety about terror. All seem to take the view that they are more likely to gain a hearing if they pursue their arguments or claims through the prism of security.

Businesses have systematically used concern with homeland security to win public subsidies and handouts. And, paradoxically, the critics of big business use similar tactics – many environmental activists have started linking their traditional alarmist campaigns to the public's fear of terror attacks. Leading American consumer activist Ralph Nader has warned that if an aeroplane were to hit a nuclear-power station, the subsequent meltdown could contaminate an area the 'size of Pennsylvania'. But probably the most imaginative storyline came from the Worldwatch Institute. It issued a statement entitled 'The Bioterror in Your Burger', which argued that although past attempts to clean up America's food chain had 'failed to inspire politicians', a patriotic demand for homeland security could 'finally lead to meaningful action'. The Detroit Project, a campaign started by liberal commentator Arianna Huffington and Americans for Fuel-Efficient Cars, links its campaign against sports utility vehicles (SUVs) with the war on terrorism, speaking of the need to 'free ourselves from the nations and terrorists holding us hostage through our addiction to oil'.

Some environmentalists argue that their programmes offer the most effective counter-terrorist strategy of all. In an article for the online journal *OnEarth*, David Corn, the Washington-based editor of America's left-leaning weekly *The Nation*, argued that 'technologies long challenged by environmental advocates are potential sources of immense danger in an era of terrorism'. 'Environmentalism will have to be an essential component of counter-terrorism,' he added. Even radical critics of the war in Iraq argued against the war by ratcheting up fears of terrorism. The UK's Stop the War Coalition said that a 'headlong rush into war against Iraq will precipitate the very terror threats that most sane people want to avert'. George Michael caused controversy when he released the anti-war single 'Shoot the Dog' in 2002 – but that also was an argument against war on the basis that it would make us more vulnerable to terrorism. 'I got the feeling that when it all goes off, they're gonna shoot the dog,' he sang, 'they' being the 'Mustaphas' and 'Gaza Boys' and the dog being Blair's Britain. The video that accompanied the song showed a map of Britain with a target sign across it.

There is nothing distinct about Bush's rhetoric of fear. His sentiments are echoed by leaders of other interest groups and even by his opponents. During the 2004 Presidential elections, the narrative of fear was no less important to the Kerry campaign than to his opponent. 'Kerry and his supporters are adopting president Bush's strategy of playing on the public's security fears and sometimes using incendiary charges to stoke them,' noted a prescient analysis of the 2004 election campaign.[9] Indeed, by transforming Bush into a figure that should be feared, the Democrats have proved to be the most adept cultivators of the politics of fear. While Bush has adopted a one-dimensional focus on the threat of terror, Kerry succeeded in promoting fear on several fronts. The Democrats claimed that if Bush was re-elected he would conspire to reintroduce a military draft, and turn the world into a more dangerous place. 'Despite a lot of rhetoric, Bush has failed to provide adequate homeland security,' stated one Democrat website. The message, in short, was that the security of the US depended on the election of Kerry. During the campaign, Kerry also took the opportunity to transform the shortage of flu vaccines into a scare story. He seized upon this issue and declared that Bush could not be trusted with protecting the public's health. His intervention provoked a panic; people who hadn't previously heard about the flu vaccine started queuing up to receive it.

Many critics of the politics of fear only recognize it in its most grotesque form. They frequently apply a double standard for assessing who uses fear as a political weapon. Bush appears to be judged by a different standard to Kerry. When critics of Bush resort to transmitting scare stories they regard it as an act of raising awareness and not of promoting fear. Yet many radical

activists are no less promiscuous in their use of the rhetoric of
terror than Bush. Thus they write of the terror experienced by
poor Americans who lack access to health insurance or the terror
experienced through racist policies on minorities. According to
one critic, 'terrorism also includes what can be called the
"terrorism of everyday life", manifest, in part, through the
suffering and hardships experienced by millions of adults and
children who lack adequate food, health care, jobs, retirement
funds and basic living quarters'.[10] In this attempt to subvert the
dominant rhetoric of war on terror, critics try to shift the focus of
the problem and inadvertently lend credibility to it.

During the 2004 election campaign, radical opponents of the
Republican administration had little inhibition about inventing
their brand of scare stories. 'Only Ralph Nader appears to be
fully awake to the peril,' wrote radical American commentator
Mike Davis in an article entitled 'The monster at the door'.[11] The
monster peril in question was H5N1, the lethal avian influenza
virus that first emerged in Hong Kong in 1997. At the outset of
the American Presidential election campaign, Nader wrote to
warn George W. Bush that 'The Big One' was coming, and to
urge a 'presidential conference on influenza epidemics and
pandemics' to confront 'the looming threats to the health of
millions of people'. Davis quoted official estimates that a new flu
pandemic would infect 40 to 400 million Americans: 'multiply
that by a 70 per cent kill rate and ponder your family's future'.
'Ironically,' wrote Davis, 'in our "culture of fear"' dominated by
the fear of bioterrorism, 'the least attention is given to the threat
that is truly most threatening'.

The difference between old radicals like Nader and Davis and
their opponents is that the former prefer scaremongering about
flu to terrorist alerts 'because this allows them to ride a number
of hobbyhorses – about the factory-farming conditions alleged to
foster avian flu, about drug companies' lack of interest in
producing low-profit vaccines, about complacent governments

and about the impoverished communities in developing countries that are likely to bear the brunt of any epidemic'.[12]

Fear has become the common currency of claims in general. Health activists, environmentalists and advocacy groups are no less involved in using scare stories to pursue their agenda than politicians devoted to getting the public's attention through inciting anxieties about crime and law and order. In fact the narrative of fear has become so widely assimilated that it is now self-consciously expressed in a personalized and privatized way. In previous eras where the politics of fear had a powerful grasp – in Latin American dictatorships, Fascist Italy or Stalin's Soviet Union – people rarely saw fear as an issue in its own right. Rather, they were frightened that what happened to a friend or neighbour might also happen to them. They were not preoccupied with fear as a problem in an abstract sense. Today, however, public fears are rarely expressed in response to any specific event. Rather, the politics of fear captures a sensibility towards life in general. The statement 'I am frightened' is rarely focused on something specific, but tends to express a diffuse sense of powerlessness. Or fears are expressed in the form of a complaint about an individual, such as 'Bush really scares me' or 'he's a scary president'. Ironically, in the very act of denouncing Bush's politics of fear, the complainant advances his or her own version of the same perspective by pointing out how terrifying the President apparently is.

As I argued previously in my book *Culture of Fear: Risk Taking and the Morality of Low Expectation*, fear has become a powerful force that dominates the public imagination. This was the case for some time before 9/11, and its ascendancy has not been predicated on the issue of terrorism. Its defining feature is the belief that humanity is confronted by powerful destructive forces that threaten our everyday existence. The line that used to delineate reality from science fiction has become blurred. So government officials have looked into the alleged threat posed by killer asteroids to human survival; some scientists warn that an influenza pandemic is around the corner; others claim that 'time is running out' for the human race unless we do something about global warming. 'The end is nigh' is no longer a warning issued by religious fanatics; rather, scaremongering is represented as the act of a concerned and responsible citizen.

Advocacy groups often claim that we are not scared enough and that the public should be more 'aware' of the risks they face. Newspapers compete with one another in the promotion of different scare stories, whether it's Frankenstein foods, the risks posed by the MMR vaccine, economy-flight syndrome, or asylum seekers. The prevalence of such scare stories suggests that society feels uncomfortable with itself. It cannot discuss any problem without going into panic mode. Overnight we discover that obesity is an 'epidemic' and is likely to kill more people than smoking does. Discussions about new technology, drugs, health or the environment invariably focus on worst-case scenarios. The cumulative impact is to transform fear into a cultural perspective through which society makes sense of itself. Despite appearances, such fear is not finally limited to specific issues but is about everything. The culture of fear is underpinned by a profound sense of powerlessness, a diminished sense of agency that leads people to turn themselves into passive subjects who can only complain, 'we are frightened'.

Politics has internalized the culture of fear. So political disagreements are often over which risk the public should worry about the most. Politics in Europe is currently dominated by debates about the fear of terror, the fear of asylum seekers, the fear of anti-social behaviour, fears over children, fears concerning food, fear about health, fear for the environment, fear for our pensions, fears over the future of Europe. In the United States, too, politicians vie with one another about which fears to promote. Voters have a choice: whether to fear Bush, Kerry, terrorists, crime, the poor quality of health services, pollution or a variety of other threats. The politics of fear appears to transcend even fundamental differences in opinion.

And yet the politics of fear could not flourish if it did not resonate so powerfully with today's cultural climate. Politicians cannot simply create fear from thin air. Nor do they monopolize the deployment of fear; panics about health or security can just as easily begin on the Internet or through the efforts of an advocacy group as from the efforts of government spin doctors. Paradoxically, governments spend as much time trying to contain the effects of spontaneously generated scare stories as they do pursuing their own fear campaigns. The reason why the politics of fear has such a powerful resonance is because of the way that personhood has been recast as the vulnerable subject. In an era where the ethos of 'there is no alternative' prevails, there is little need for an omnipotent state to remind us of our lack of power. The state of diminished agency is one that disposes people to interpret events through the prism of anxiety and fear. And if vulnerability is indeed the defining feature of the human condition, we are quite entitled to fear everything.

The politicization of fear

Although the politics of fear reflects a wider cultural mood, it did not emerge spontaneously on its own accord. Fear has been consciously politicized. Throughout history fear has been deployed as a political weapon by the ruling elites. Machiavelli's advice to rulers that they will find 'greater security in being feared than in being loved' has been heeded by successive generations of authoritarian governments. Fear can be employed to coerce, terrorize and maintain public order. Through provoking a common reaction to a perceived threat it can also provide a focus for gaining consensus and unity. Today, the objective of the politics of fear is to gain consensus and to forge a measure of unity around an otherwise disconnected elite. But whatever the intentions of its authors, *its main effect is to enforce the idea that there is no alternative.*

It is in the writings of the English philosopher Thomas Hobbes that we find the first systematic attempt to develop a politics of fear that can be utilized to enforce the idea that there is no alternative. For Hobbes, one of the principal objectives of the cultivation of fear was to neutralize any radical impulse towards social experimentation. To achieve this objective, Hobbes argued that people had to be persuaded that 'the less they dare, the better it is both for commonwealth and for themselves'.[13] Those who internalized a consciousness of fear were unlikely to engage in risk taking and social experimentation. The promotion of an expansive consciousness of aversion to the unknown would also help to make people afraid of that 'which they never experienced as harmful'. Today, this fear of 'unknowable harm' has been institutionalized and underpins the prevailing culture of fear. In Hobbes' time matters were very different. Instead of the ethos of 'there is no alternative' he confronted a climate where at least significant sections of society were pursuing revolutionary change. Plunged into a civil war by a movement led by bold visionaries, Hobbes regarded the politics of fear as the precondition for the consolidation of order and stability.

Today, the ruling elites do not have to construct fear artificially. Thanks to the exhaustion of politics, this sentiment is already embedded within society. The question that confronts public figures is whether they should seek to minimize or politicize fear. This was a question that confronted Philip Gould, a former campaign adviser to New Labour. In a document titled 'Fighting the Fear Factor' published in February 1994, Gould observed that,

Modern electorates are insecure, uncertain and anxious. They 'are more afraid of things getting worse than they are hopeful of things getting better'. This mood of anxiety about the future allowed the right to use the tactics of fear, enabling them to dominate politics for the 1980s and early 1990s. To defend against attacks rooted in fear, progressive parties had to respond instantly when challenged.[14]

Gould did not spell out what he thought about the politics of fear. But as Heartfield noted, the logic of his argument was that Labour, too, had to create its 'own fear factor' if it was to be re-elected.[15] As subsequent events demonstrate, New Labour could not resist the temptation to embrace the politics of fear. From Blair's 1997 election slogan 'tough on crime, tough on the causes of crime' to his promise in the 2005 campaign that a third New Labour Government would bring about a 'step change in the fight against crime and disorder', events show that Gould's insights have been well assimilated.[16]

During and after the 2004 American Presidential election, many Democrats adopted a posture similar to that of Gould. For example, Don Hazen, the executive editor of online publication *AlterNet*, warned that the 'fear factor is often overlooked by progressives, who frequently make appeals to logic on the assumption that if people know all the facts they will act accordingly'. Hazen felt that 'intellectual arguments' are 'not at their most potent at this juncture' and therefore 'facts and analysis must be accompanied by a vision that addresses safety'.[17] In other words, 'progressives', too, must learn to make the fear factor work for them.

The politicization of fear is inextricably linked to the process of exhaustion and demoralization noted before. Societies that are able to project a positive vision of the future do not need to employ fear as a currency in public life. Politicians that attempt to mobilize the electorate around a positive programme of action tend to eschew the politics of fear. President Franklin D. Roosevelt's inaugural address in 1933 offered a sense of future possibilities. His statement that the 'only thing we have to Fear is Fear itself' was integral to a positive future orientation which would eventually lead to the launching of the New Deal. The contrast between Roosevelt's message and the statements made by politicians today is striking. The message currently transmitted is 'Not If – But When'. This statement regarding the threat of terrorism, which assumes the form of a 'sensible' warning, directly encourages a sense of resignation concerning the inevitability of something bad happening.

There is now a substantial body of opinion that regards fear as a positive asset for gaining a moral consensus in society. In its contemporary form, the politics of fear was most coherently elucidated by the Harvard political theorist Judith Shklar. Shklar argued for what she calls the 'liberalism of fear' because, at a time of terror, it can unite people against cruelty and injustice. 'Because the fear of systematic cruelty is so universal, moral claims based on its prohibition have an immediate appeal and can gain recognition without much argument,' she notes. Her position reflects the belief that in contemporary times what can motivate people is not a positive vision of future possibilities but the fear of evil. According to this perspective, it is the fear of cruelty that constitutes the moral basis for liberalism. She remarks that:

> It does not to be sure offer a *summum bonum* toward which all political agents should strive, but it certainly does begin with a *summum malum*, which all of us know and would avoid if only we could. That evil is cruelty and the fear it inspires, and the very fear of fear itself.[18]

Avoiding terror and cruelty is presented as the basis for a public ethos that could override division and fragmentation and enjoy widespread support. Whatever the issues that divide society, our dislike of terror, cruelty, genocide and suffering appears as the foundation around which a sense of common purpose can be crafted.

Shklar's contribution provides a coherent attempt to bypass the problem represented by the absence of morally purposeful politics through orchestrating a consensus against the things that we fear and dread. Western society has whole-heartedly embraced this paradigm. Over the past quarter of a century Western culture has developed an expansive consciousness of genocide, cruelty and terror. What in previous times would have been diagnosed as instances of political violence, brutality and terror are routinely translated into a new sensation-seeking vocabulary of genocide, ethnic cleansing, Holocaust or crimes against humanity. It appears that, periodically, the Western imagination requires to familiarize itself with unbounded horror to remind itself of its moral purpose. As Robin noted, the battle against ethnic cleansing and other horrors over 'there' has been seized upon as an opportunity to forge both a 'progressive' and 'conservative' renewal.[19]

The tendency to regard fear as possessing considerable potential for supporting social solidarity and moral renewal has a powerful presence within the cultural and political elites. The Holocaust has been turned into an all-purpose symbol that is regularly used by campaigners to support a variety of different causes. As Jeffrey Alexander, one of America's most influential sociologists, notes, in the 1980s 'the engorged, free-floating Holocaust symbol became analogically associated with the movement against nuclear power and nuclear testing and, more generally, with the ecological movements that emerged at the time'. Rather than interpreting this trend as yet another example of the trivialization of the Holocaust, Alexander believes that this is an instance of employing a 'powerful bridging metaphor to make sense of social life'.[20] The dread of this symbol of evil, he claims, may lead to the construction of a positive moral universal.

The belief that social solidarity is far more likely to be forged around a reaction against the bad than around the aspiration for the good exercises a strong influence over politicians, opinion makers and academics. Instead of being concerned about the destructive consequences of the mood of anxiety and fear that afflicts the public, many social theorists regard these as sentiments that can be harnessed for the purpose of forging social cohesion. The German sociologist Ulrich Beck believes that the threat of global terrorism has this potential. He believes that 'in an age where trust and faith in God, class, nation and progress have largely disappeared humanity's common fear has proved the last – ambivalent – resource for making new bonds'.[21] The transformation of 'humanity's common fear' into a positive asset is underpinned by a pessimistic prognosis that accepts the irrevocable loss of trust in progress and enlightenment. Unfortunately, the attempt to turn fear into a positive asset has the effect of normalizing it.

In the UK, Beck's approach is forcefully advocated by the sociologist Anthony Giddens. Giddens self-consciously attempts to reframe people's fear into a resource for moral renewal. He is distinctly upbeat about this project, claiming that 'this is probably the first time in history that we can speak of the emergence of universal values'. Why? Because these values are now driven by the 'heuristic of fear' as we confront the 'threats which humanity has created for itself'.[22] Following on from Shklar, he offers the 'negative utopia' of uniting around the 'bads'.[23] The tendency to offer fear as the negative moral foundation for community renewal is underwritten by the assumption that a positive vision of the future can no longer provide the focus for the construction of a social consensus.

In the US, some intellectuals around the Democratic Party believe that the liberal-left needs to connect with the politics of fear if it is to make headway. Michael Walzer, co-editor of the periodical *Dissent*, believes that 'fear has to be our starting point, even though it is a passion most easily exploited by the right'. Echoing Hobbes, Walzer argues that protecting people from the fear of death is a 'legitimate and necessary task', and he proposes a version of the politics of fear that is more 'progressive' than that practised by Bush. 'The Bush administration exploits our fear, but it is not interested in a collective effort to cope with them – that is, to provide the necessary forms of protection and to stimulate the necessary forms of mutual assistance,' he writes. Walzer believes that a synthesis of the politics of fear with an enlightened social agenda represents the way forward for the liberal-left.[24]

It is important to realize that the representation of fear as an instrument of solidarity does not simply mean an accommodation to the existing state of affairs. It also represents a call for its perpetuation. From this perspective, scaring the public is represented as an act of civic responsibility. For example, the American political scientist George Marcus asserts that anxiety assists individuals to be more informed citizens. 'Most Americans do not know very much about politics in general or where candidates for office stand on the sundry issues of the day,' he argues. But, he adds, 'anxious citizens are well informed because the emotional incentives have caused them to grasp the importance of issues in uncertain times'.[25]

Marcus' idealization of the benefits of anxiety is a sentiment that is widely shared. The management of public anxiety is now systematically pursued by public officials and campaigns dedicated to the task of 'raising awareness'. In a cultural climate where fear has become both politicized and normalized, campaigners committed to raising awareness do not simply exaggerate, they self-consciously promote what they consider to be 'good lies'. For many years, AIDS-awareness campaigners refused to acknowledge that in Western societies this disease was not a significant threat to most heterosexuals. Many supporters of this campaign remain unapologetic about the utilization of dishonest propaganda. Writing in the *Guardian*, Mark Lawson declared, 'the Government has lied, and I am glad'. Yes, the Government promoted 'exaggerations and inaccuracies' but so what – this was a case of a 'good' lie.[26]

The defence of the 'good lie' or the 'greater truth' is invoked when the inflated stories peddled by campaigners devoted to raising awareness are exposed to the public. 'Children will die before their parents', warned the British House of Commons Health Select Committee report on obesity in 2004. To raise awareness of this danger, the report highlighted the case of a three-year-old girl, who was presented as the youngest known death from obesity due to her parents' failure to feed her properly. When her doctor complained this was a lie, the girl's obesity being a result of a genetic defect, some advocates of the report refused to apologize. As far as they were concerned it was legitimate to make small mistakes in the interest of a greater truth. A similar approach is adopted by some campaigners committed to raising awareness about global warming. Stephen Schneider, a climatologist, justified the distortion of evidence in the following terms: 'Because we are not just scientists but human beings as well ... we need to ... capture the public imagination.' He added that 'we have to offer up scary scenarios, make simplified dramatic statements, and make little mention of any doubts that we have'.[27] His colleague David Viner takes a similar approach. Noting that the film *The Day After Tomorrow* 'got a lot of the detail wrong' he excuses this on the ground that anything which 'raises awareness about climate change must be a good thing'.[28]

The renunciation of politics

In an important study titled *Fear: The History of a Political Idea*, Corey Robin rightly draws attention to a situation where 'fear often serves as a ground for intellectuals in need of grounding arguments'. He adds that 'at moments of doubt about the ability of positive principles to animate moral perception or inspire public action, fear has seemed an ideal source of political insight and energy'.[29] Robin is concerned that a significant group of American intellectuals advance arguments that are legitimated through sensitizing the public to a species of fear. He rightly notes that 'we must abandon the notion that fear can be the foundation of political life'.[30]

Unfortunately, fear often serves as the foundation for public discourse, and its promotion is not confined to right-wing hawks banging on their war drums. As noted previously, critics of 'the politics of fear' are often directly involved in alarmist claims. They have made a powerful contribution to the creation of a situation where mundane matters such as children's health, food or the quality of air are regular topics for scare stories. Fear has turned into a perspective that citizens share across the political divide. Indeed, the main distinguishing feature of different parties and movements is what they fear the most: the degradation of the environment, irresponsible corporates, immigrants, paedophiles, crimes, global warming or weapons of mass destruction.

In contemporary times, fear migrates freely from one problem to the next without there being any necessity for causal or logical connection. When, in June 2002, the Southern Baptist leader Reverend Jerry Vines declared that Mohammad was a 'demon possessed pedophile' and that Allah leads Muslims to terrorism, he was simply taking advantage of the logical leaps permitted by the free-floating character of our fear narratives.[31] This arbitrary association of terrorism and paedophilia can have the effect of amplifying our fear of both. The same procedure is adopted when genetically modified products are stigmatized as Frankenstein food. Politics seems only to come alive in the caricatured form of a panic.

In one sense the term 'politics of fear' is a misnomer. Although promoted by parties and advocacy groups, it expresses the renunciation of politics. Unlike the politics of fear pursued by authoritarian regimes and dictatorships, it has no clearly focused objective other than to express claims in a language that enjoys a wider cultural resonance. Possibly one of the distinct features of our time is not the cultivation of fear but the cultivation of our sense of vulnerability. Whilst it lacks a clearly formulated objective, the cumulative impact of the politics of fear is to reinforce society's consciousness of vulnerability. And the more powerless we feel the more we are likely to find it difficult to resist the siren call of fear.

The precondition for effectively countering the politics of fear is to challenge the association of personhood with the state of vulnerability. Anxieties about uncertainty become magnified and overwhelm us when we regard ourselves as essentially vulnerable. Yet the human imagination possesses a formidable capacity to engage and learn from the risks it faces. Throughout history, humanity has learnt from its setbacks and losses and has developed ways of systematically identifying, evaluating, selecting and implementing options for reducing risks. There is always an alternative, and whether or not we are aware of the choices confronting us depends on whether we regard ourselves as defined by our vulnerability or our capacity to be resilient.

Cultivating the vulnerability of people is the main accomplish-
ment of the politics of fear. Governments now treat citizens as
vulnerable subjects who need to be treated as individuals and
who tend not to know what is in their best interest. As a result,
policy makers have shifted their attention from the public to the
private sphere.

The exhaustion of politics has channelled energies once
devoted to it towards the colonization of everyday life. The
flip-side of the depoliticization of public life is the tendency to
politicize the minutiae of people's existence. As a result, issues
that were previously unheard of as subjects of controversy can
arbitrarily dominate the headlines and then disappear. That is
why, out of the blue, the question of what food children eat
during their school lunch could erupt into a major pre-election
issue in Britain in 2005. Almost overnight, people's frustrations
and emotions were absorbed by the public performance that
surrounded the 'debate' about school dinners.

Governments are continually embarking on crusades that
target people's diets, health, sex life, parenting strategies, alcohol
consumption and attitudes and behaviour towards others. The
politicization of individual lifestyles is inversely proportional to
the depoliticization of public life. Consequently, the paradigm of
public policy has shifted from engaging with responsible citizens
to treating them as if they are biologically mature children. In the
Reagan-Thatcher years there was a distinct trend towards turning
the citizen into a customer. In more recent times this decline in

the status of the responsible citizen has accelerated and given way to a model that infantilizes people as clients or patients or as vulnerable individuals in need of support.

Unable to envision a strategy for change in the public sphere, the political elites have opted for the management of micro issues. Numerous technical matters that were never the provenance of officialdom have unexpectedly become the focus for government initiatives. The UK Government is now concerned that its clients may be 'lacking in the knowledge, skills or cooking equipment necessary to prepare healthy meals'.[1] These days, politicians are far more likely to hold strong views about the early learning of children, classroom size, the diet of their constituents or hospital waiting lists than about the future of manufacturing industry or the EU's agricultural policy. Most politicians no longer even pretend to show any interest in promoting a distinct philosophy or an ambitious project. Instead they seem preoccupied with banal 'lifestyle' issues and petty schemes for intervening in people's private affairs. In March 2005, the US Congress passed a law to keep Terri Schiavo, a brain-damaged woman, alive after a Florida judge allowed her feeding tube to be removed at her husband's request. Amid great publicity, the US President, George W. Bush, broke off his holiday to return to Washington to sign the necessary documentation. Such an exceptional procedure, normally deployed only at times of national emergency, was used to symbolize the seriousness with which Congress regards its role of policing people's personal life. The role of US and UK governments used to be associated with upholding a broad set of values, traditions and institutions, defined respectively as the American and British way of life. Nowadays, they seem much more interested in preaching to people about how they should conduct their private affairs.

In the US, the Clinton administration, like its Republican successor, regarded the sphere of family life as an important site for government activity. In May 2000, an entire White House conference was devoted to informing the public that teenagers need the guidance and support of their parents. In case some American citizens failed to grasp this point, Hillary Clinton announced that the National Partnership for Women and Families, along with the Families and Work Institute, would 'lead a campaign to promote the importance of spending time with teenagers'.[2] At the summit, politicians were free with folksy advice about the need for 'parents to take stock of their lives and work habits and look for ways to make time for their children'. 'Sitting down to dinner can have an enormously positive impact,' declared the then President Clinton. One contributor, Dorothy Strickland, took it upon herself to offer the following tips to parents and grandparents:

1. Talk with your child.
2. Listen to your child.
3. Sing and chant nursery rhymes and childhood songs you remember.
4. Turn ordinary, everyday trips into interesting excursions.
5. Play language games with your child.[3]

The condescending mode adopted by Strickland is characteristic of the way that public authorities communicate with parents. It is worth noting that the practice of subjecting the public to patronizing sermons about how to behave as parents has been vigorously embraced by New Labour, whose much-vaunted Sure Start programme self-consciously seeks to socialize mothers and fathers into its version of parenthood.

Nor do the political elites confine themselves to preaching. The most important sphere of policy innovation is driven by the objective of managing and changing how individuals live their lives. In March 2005, Britain's Secretary of State for Health, John Reid, announced government plans for a 'healthier and fitter' nation. The plans involved getting experts to 'draw up personal health plans for life' for children. An army of Orwellian-sounding community matrons will descend on schools to provide advice to 'support' children to lead healthier lifestyles. And yes, children will be given pedometers so that they can measure how far they walk in an attempt to encourage them to take more exercise.[4] Nor are adults left out of the frame. Apparently, a magazine titled *FIT*, targeting young men, will be launched, which will raise awareness on issues such as wearing condoms and losing weight. Reid also announced that a propaganda campaign will be launched 'to build public awareness and change behaviour' in areas such as obesity, sexual health and smoking. To help realize the objective of changing behaviour, the 'independent' National Consumer Council will be charged with developing 'social marketing strategy that promotes health'. This organization will 'consider health psychology and social research to determine how best to influence lifestyle and change behaviour'.

It is evident that John Reid is concerned not simply with providing information. He is in the business of behaviour modification. Instead of tackling vital national issues and their international context, his concern is solely with research that can help officials influence and alter individual behaviour. Once upon a time, such research was characterized as propaganda, and social marketing as a form of emotional manipulation. Today, emotional manipulation is represented as an instrument for 'raising awareness'. As Paul Barker, former editor of *New Society*, wrote: '[the British Government is] wedded to social intervention, for which a better phrase would be social manipulation'.[5] So is the US Congress. A quick search of the US Congress' 2005 legislative agenda shows that 50 bills refer to the words 'behaviour' and 'health'. Bills such as the 'Health Promotion FIRST Act', introduced in the Senate, seek to politicize behaviour.

The assumption that government has the duty and right to manage and alter personal behaviour is a relatively new development. Certainly governments have always sought to influence public behaviour, but they have tended to rely on local custom, moral norms and the informal pressures of community life to do so. In democratic societies there used to be an unwritten rule that government should not intrude into the domain of people's private lives. This point was at least rhetorically acknowledged in the UK Government's 1998 consultation document, *Supporting Families*. 'Governments have to be very careful in devising policies that affect our most intimate relationships,' it warned.[6] Despite its note of caution, however, *Supporting Families* moved brazenly into areas that directly affect intimate aspects of family life. It outlined the intention of Government to initiate a programme for helping people to prepare for marriage, and proposed various projects oriented towards saving marriages. It also mooted policies directed at helping parents cope with the arrival of a baby, and, on a more ominous note, suggested imposing parenting orders on mothers and fathers who are deemed to have failed to control their children. Since the publication of this document, the Government has adopted a highly interventionist stance. Former Home Secretary Jack Straw stated that the culture of parenting needs to be changed so that 'seeking advice and help' is 'seen not as failure but as the actions of concerned and responsible parents'. One of his objectives was to turn parenting into a legitimate sphere for government intervention.[7]

The loss of restraint towards intervention in people's private affairs is one of the most significant developments in the sphere of public policy during the past two decades. Governments, which have become uncertain of values and their purpose, have refocused their energies towards the management of individual behaviour and the regulation of informal relationships. Increasingly, they have sought to adopt the role of protecting people from themselves and from other members of the public. In return for people acknowledging the authority of government to play the role of a caring Big Brother, the state is happy to provide support and affirmation to individuals in search of recognition.

Behaviour modification

Government and its agencies have little inhibition about using scare tactics to achieve the objective of behaviour modification. One of the distinct motifs of such propaganda is the risk that lurks in people's informal life. Take a recent London Police advertising campaign aimed at men who hurt their domestic partners. One poster reads: 'Bad day at the office? How will you unwind? Glass of wine? Nice meal? Break your wife's jaw?' In case anyone missed the message, another poster asks: 'When was the last time you told your girlfriend you love her? Was it just after you nearly killed her?'[8] The attitude of contempt towards grown-up men communicated by these ads is far from unusual. Such sentiments are continually recycled through government advertising campaigns.

Take the UK Government-sponsored publication, *Married Life: A Rough Guide for Couples Today*. It offers paternalistic advice on how to buy a wedding ring and on how couples should communicate with each other. Readers are advised to allocate time for each partner to speak in turn and without interruption. The way the pamphlet is written conveys the assumption that couples who are about to get married are actually children playing at being grown-ups. It assumes that readers lack common sense and the resources to make elementary decisions about how to conduct their intimate affairs. Worse still, *Married Life* promotes the idea that it possesses a superior understanding of human relationships, which it has a duty to impart to an otherwise immature public. The same patronizing formula is adopted by a booklet *Dads & Sons*, published in August 2002 by the Department of Education and Skills. In a section advising fathers how to help sons with their homework, it states, 'make sure he's got somewhere comfortable to work away from the TV'. *Dads & Sons* assumes that fathers are just grown-up children who need to be reminded of the blindingly obvious.

Not all government publications or initiatives that target the domain of privacy seek overtly to treat grown-ups as children. But they tend be based on the premise that they have both the right and the authority to modify people's personal behaviour. From time to time, government officials react defensively when criticized for overstepping their jurisdiction and expanding the Nanny State. Their usual reaction is to assert that what they are doing is not to promote the Nanny State but to 'help' or 'support' the targets of its intervention. However, with the passing of time, advocates of state intrusion into private life have become more aggressive in justifying their right to manage people's behaviour. It was in this vein that Children's Minister Margaret Hodge insisted that the government has a 'powerful' role to play in family life. She argued that 'it's not a question of whether we should intrude in family life, but how and when – and we have to constantly remain focused on our purpose: to strengthen and support families so that they can enjoy their opportunities and help provide opportunities for their children'.[9]

The rhetoric of 'support' is frequently used to justify policies that demand that people conform to the government's norms. 'Support' is always extended to those whom the government considers to be in need of help – whether they like it or not. Support rarely means assisting people to improve what they are already struggling to do. In practice, it means placing pressure on people to adopt a course of action favoured by government. 'Promote health by influencing people's attitudes to the choices they make,' is how one government strategy document puts it.[10] Supporting people to make choices actually means getting people to do what government believes is in their best interest. From the standpoint of this paternalistic vocabulary, informed choice means the adoption of behaviour that is informed by government-sanctioned values.

Behind the scenes, the political elites are involved in a continuous crusade to gain public acceptance for their project of colonizing people's private world. Publicity campaigns, 'research' and surveys are mobilized to endow this project with legitimacy. So it is not surprising that surveys regularly echo this approach and insist that the public wants to be treated like children. Take a survey published by the King's Fund in June 2004. This organization, devoted to raising 'awareness' of public health issues, claimed that, of a thousand people surveyed, most favoured the idea of a Nanny State influencing such matters as diet and smoking in public. 'This poll goes a long way to debunking the myth that the public are afraid of a "nanny state",' commented King's Fund chief executive Niall Dickson.[11] Surveys which 'inform' the public about what it really wants are integral to the process of transforming grown-up people into needy children.

It is important to note that the trend towards intervention in private life is very different to the previous approach to health and social policy. Supporters of the project of colonizing the private sphere sometime claim that their policies simply continue the progressive tradition that has seen the abolishing of child labour or the provision of school milk. They claim that their policies are designed to avoid problems that can compromise public health. However, defenders of the Nanny State confuse public health policies that seek to create conditions for healthy living with those that attempt to manage individual behaviour and manipulate people's emotions. Campaigns for 'healthier lifestyles' are less about improving our health than about directing how we ought to live. They are motivated by what some supporters of the idea characterize as the *politics of behaviour*. According to a prominent New Labour Minister, Tessa Jowell, managing 'the new politics of behaviour' is 'one of the most fascinating challenges facing the government'.[12]

Unlike Jowell, most advocates of state management of personal life have not yet codified their attitude as the 'politics of behaviour'. Nevertheless, it is evident that behaviour management has gradually turned into an undeclared project favoured by the political elites. The term 'politics of behaviour' was coined by Labour MP Frank Field, who argues that Britain is moving from the 'politics of class to the politics of behaviour'.[13] Field believes that the 'new politics is about moderating behaviour and re-establishing the social virtues of self-discipline' and it centres on 'reinforcing what is good and acceptable behaviour'.[14] Field's usage of the term was primarily developed to deal with anti-social neighbours, but for others its focus is the management of people's lifestyles and informal relationships.[15]

Some proponents of the politics of behaviour prefer the term 'positive welfare' to describe their policies. For Giddens, such policies both pre-empt problems and help alter lifestyles that contribute to negative outcomes. So it is not simply sufficient to prevent smoking – 'treatment for the physical effects of smoking needs to be geared to making sure that individuals subsequently alter their lifestyle habits'.[16] Unable to change the circumstances that cry out for decisive social policy, the promoters of the politics of behaviour attempt to alter individual lifestyle. As Christopher Lasch argued in his critique of therapeutic politics, the state bureaucracy seeks to transform 'collective grievances into personal problems amenable to therapeutic intervention'.[17]

I feel your pain

The reorientation of the Welfare State towards attending to the therapeutic needs of the public is endorsed by some critics of traditional redistributionist social policy. They claim that, in the past, the traditional policy was far too focused on material goods. The argument for a more emotional system of welfare is generally pursued on the ground that a 'holistic' approach is needed, one that meets the 'emotional as well as physical needs of human beings'.[18] This approach has received an intellectual boost from the claim that social inequalities are experienced through 'psychosocial mechanisms' linking structure to individual health. It is argued that socio-economic factors now primarily affect health through indirect psychosocial rather than direct material routes. From this standpoint, the call for an egalitarian society is justified on the grounds that it contributes to the best mental and physical health. 'Emotions, health and distributive justice are therefore intimately related in the developed Western world,' argues one advocate of this approach.[19] There is a significant body of opinion within the field of British social policy that actually regards the assumption of the therapeutic role of the state as a long overdue reform. Paul Hoggett argues that the 'concept of "well-being" provides a core principle around which a new vision of positive welfare could be organized'. For Hoggett and his co-thinkers, 'well-being is defined essentially in mental-health terms'.[20] Writing in the same vein, Richard Layard claims that public policy should be oriented towards making society happier. And 'to become happier, we have to change our inner attitudes as much as our outward circumstances', he observes.[21]

The representation of state intervention in the internal life of people as an essentially unobjectionable, even desirable, process enjoys widespread intellectual support. From this perspective, the role of public authority and of the therapeutic professional is an empowering one. On both sides of the Atlantic, advocacy groups continually demand that government embraces policies that promote 'emotional intelligence', 'happiness', 'emotional democracy' or 'emotional literacy'. The aim of the British think-tank Antidote is to integrate the insights of psychology into political and public life. It seeks to advocate policies that aim to 'foster emotional attitudes tending to support the development of more cohesive societies'.[22] According to Frank Scott, a professor in public administration at San Francisco State University, therapeutic governance is concerned with 'reuniting the self that modernism has sought to split apart'.[23] Supporters of therapeutic governance are not particularly bothered about the implications of assigning responsibility for 'reuniting the self' to the bureaucratic institutions of the state.

It may well be that the politics of behaviour provides a provisional solution for an oligarchy that is confused about its role and direction. This approach substitutes therapeutic intervention for political direction. Today's cultural elite may lack confidence in telling people what to believe but it feels quite comfortable about instructing people how and what to feel. This shift from politics to the personal is one of the distinctive features of public life. As public life becomes emptied of its content, private and personal preoccupations have been projected into the public sphere. Consequently, passions that were once stirred by ideological differences are far more likely to be engaged by individual misbehaviour, private troubles and personality conflicts. In this climate, the practice of individual therapy is seen as indistinguishable from the measures that are required for the 'healing' of society. When Blair or Clinton indicate that 'I feel your pain,' they are offering empathy through assuming the role of the politician-therapist. Public institutions have also adopted this orientation towards the management of emotion.

What commentators describe as the Nanny State is more accurately described as the therapeutic state.[24] Therapeutic policies aim to forge a relationship between government and individuals through the management of the internal lives of people. As one commentator noted, 'it is telling that technologies similar to those employed by counselling have now become part and parcel of the way in which the current British Government governs its people'. The politics of behaviour represents a quest to 'gain unfettered access to people's subjectivity'.[25] Managing people's emotions is an essential component of an outlook that believes that changing people's attitudes is an important business of government. Of course to some extent governments have always sought to influence the public's attitude, but doing so in relation to going to war or the issue of capital punishment is very different to the project of manipulating how individuals behave within the confines of their home. This therapeutic turn to the private individual conveyed through the politics of behaviour is underwritten by the idea that people 'need support' in order to cope with their state of vulnerability. Treating citizens as vulnerable children constitutes the unstated supposition of the politics of behaviour.

The representation of therapeutic governance as essentially unproblematic and potentially even empowering is underwritten by cultural norms that possess a relatively weak sense of individual capacity. This is an outlook that finds it difficult to accept the ideal of the self-determining subject capable of exercising democratic citizenship. Viewing individual subjectivity as feeble is the flip-side of this new form of statist intellectual outlook. It represents scepticism concerning people's ability to act as responsible citizens, without the support of professionals who know what is in their best interest. The anti-democratic ethos – discussed in the previous chapters – informs the practices adopted by government institutions. People are not so much engaged as 'treated', 'supported' or 'counselled'. What has emerged as the prevailing paradigm is a highly individualized orientation towards the public that seeks to disaggregate them and manage them as clients or patients. Of course, as long as the public is disengaged from politics they can be treated as atomized individuals. The politics of behaviour both confirms this status and consolidates it.

The representation of state policy as an instrument of empowerment recasts the dependent relationship of the patient to the therapist in a disturbing institutional form. It is difficult to reconcile the view of an individual as someone whose emotional well-being is contingent on institutional support with the democratic vision of a citizen who holds the powers that be to account. The transformation of the citizen into a patient has the potential for altering the relationship between the people and the public institutions of society. As Vanessa Pupavac, in her critique of therapeutic governance, argues, the 'redrawing of the citizen and state relationship has been accompanied by the erosion of the social contract conceptualisation of the citizen as an autonomous rational subject'.[26] The new therapeutic social contract is underwritten by the paternalistic assumption that the vulnerable subject needs the management and 'support' of officialdom and the state. Indeed, in all but name it ceases to be a social contract and turns the relationship between the public and the state into an individual transaction.

It's coercive implications aside, the policy of behaviour modification contributes to the consolidation of political disengagement. It encourages people to dwell on their personal and private troubles and to regard themselves as lacking agency. It incites people to regard themselves as objects, rather than as subjects of their destiny. People who are encouraged to conduct their lives without the support of public agencies are unlikely to possess the capacity to behave as responsible citizens. The low expectations that the elite has of the public directly contribute to people lowering their expectations further. The politics of behaviour preys on people's existential fear and encourages them to acquiesce to the demands of those 'who know best'.

Thought police

It is important to realize that the politics of behaviour does not confine its ambition to regulating what people do. It is also in the business of emotion management, and ultimately it seeks to police the way people think. Of course all governments attempt to do this, striving through their authority, institutional power, propaganda and the education system to gain support for their view of the world while simultaneously seeking to undermine sentiments they oppose. However, until recent times, modern democratic governments did not seek to extend their activity into the realm of *policing* people's thoughts. It is only during the past two decades that this desire to shape people's thought has become modified by the belief that an individual's internal life is not simply a personal matter, but a legitimate subject for public concern. This trend is particularly striking in the criminal justice system, where individuals are frequently forced or pressurized into participating in therapies such as drugs treatment courses. In many states in the US, drivers convicted of an offence are compelled to attend anger-management programmes. In Britain, the early release of prisoners is conditional on attending courses in anger management, drug and alcohol addiction, or sex therapy.

However, the management of the emotions is not simply confined to the criminal justice system. *Behaviour modification has become a substitute for promoting socialization through attempting to win the arguments through reasoned debate.* This approach is made crystal clear in the UK Department of Health's Orwellian-titled document *Delivering Choosing Health: Making Healthier Choices Easier*. In this document, 'helping people make healthy choices', which is 'now at the core of mainstream activity by government', is even associated with the goal of reducing race inequalities and building social cohesion.[27] Principles upheld by the state – such as healthy lifestyle or diversity – often acquire a quasi-religious character, and are sometimes codified into an absolute value. The clearest expressions of this trend are the so-called 'hate crimes'. As the American critic Paul Piccone argues, 'so-called "hate" laws seek to homogenize internal psychological states with moral injunctions and legal structures resembling those of the Spanish Inquisition'.[28] Hate laws are oriented towards policing unacceptable forms of individual thought on the ground of protecting the emotionally vulnerable target groups from prejudice. Such laws have little practical purpose since there already exist plenty of legal means for prosecuting different forms of violence and incitement to violence. Nevertheless, they serve an important symbolic role of indicating what forms of thoughts and emotions are acceptable and which ones are beyond the pale.

The tendency towards the policing of thought superficially resembles the scenario outlined in Orwell's *Nineteen Eighty-Four*, where people's behaviour is under constant surveillance by the Thought Police. 'A party member lives from birth to death under the eye of the Thought Police,' wrote Orwell; 'his friendships, his relaxations, his behaviour towards his wife and children, the expression on his face when he is alone, the words he mutters in sleep, even the characteristic movements of his body, are all jealously scrutinised'.[29] In Orwell's novel, the Thought Police served as an instrument of totalitarian control. This was a regime that was haunted by the fear of instability and disorder. The situation today has little in common with this scenario. In contemporary times, the imperative towards policing thought is driven by the need of the elite to establish points of contact with an otherwise disaggregated public. The management of people's emotions is not focused on achieving a specific objective. Its aim is to cultivate a state of dependence for its authority. Unlike in *Nineteen Eighty-Four*, the authoritarian and coercive dimension of policing thought rarely assumes an open and public form. Such policing seeks to exercise control not through a system of punishment, but through cultivating a sense of vulnerability, powerlessness and dependence. Its objective is the internalization of the sensibility of self-limitation.

Aside from its authoritarian aspect of policing thought, the management of emotion encourages a climate of emotional correctness. For example, turning the feeling of hate into a crime contributes to the construction of an environment that is inhospitable to the free exchange or clash of ideas. An illustration of this tendency is the attempt by the UK Government to ban religious hatred through the enactment of a new law which will undermine the right to criticize religions and religious organiza-

tions. Whichever way the Government seeks to justify this
illiberal measure its effect is to close down debate on a matter
that has been a subject of controversy for centuries. 'It is right
and the state has a right to put some boundaries on free speech,'
was the cavalier manner with which Home Office Minister Fiona
Mactaggart sought to justify this authoritarian legislation.[30]

In Britain and the United States, the principle of free speech
has been put to question by those who argue that since words
hurt and can cause psychological damage, the victims should be
protected from distress. Even art has come under scrutiny. Artists
have faced censure and been forced to close down their
exhibitions on the grounds that their art offends sections of the
public. As Mick Hume, the radical British social commentator,
argues: 'you are free to think and say what you feel, so long as it
does not harm others – except that the definition of harm has
been extended to include hurting their feelings or damaging their
self-esteem'. As examples of this trend, he points out that there
are new laws on incitement to hatred, and new codes and rules
about what you can say in any and every context, from the
university seminar to the football stadium.[31]

The growing authoritarian consensus against offensive speech
exemplifies how the infantilization of the public can have such
disturbing consequences as the marginalization of nonconformist
ideas. Throughout history, any idea worth its salt has been
guaranteed to cause widespread offence. Everything from
universal suffrage to organ transplants, from contraception to
legalized divorce, was once considered an offence to standards of
public decency. Each time, the pain caused to some people proved
well worth it for the gains offered to humanity as a whole. That is
why Dr Samuel Johnson could argue that 'every man has the right
to utter what he thinks truth, and every man has a right to knock
him down for it'. This sentiment has become an anathema to a
culture that has adopted a uniquely diminished version of
subjectivity. One that assumes that people are too weak and

vulnerable to get through the rigours of life without being protected from hurtful words or images. The policing of thought saves the public the trouble of having to work out how they feel about controversial issues.

In previous times, the orientation of public institutions was directed towards promoting and enforcing acceptable forms of conduct and beliefs. Since the elite find it difficult to endow their activities with a sense of purpose they find it difficult systematically to pursue such policies. That is why they have opted for an approach that encourages conformity and dependence through the management of people's subjectivity. This approach extends the business of government from the public to the private and more disturbingly to the internal life of individuals. The demise of politics encourages a process whereby public grievances are systematically recast as private troubles susceptible to therapeutic intervention.

Conclusion: Humanizing Humanism

We need to retrace our steps to the time before there was a left and right to recover the progressive legacy of the past. We do this not because we want to escape from politics as we know it but because these are pre-political times that require the recovery of ideas through which a challenge to fatalism can be mounted. This demands that we let go of the categories that helped illuminate political life in the last century but which have now become emptied of meaning. Previously, we noted that the right has given up on the past and the left on the future – we have to re-establish a claim on both. The line of division that matters today is between those who subscribe to the conformist embrace of the present and those who want to mobilize the past achievements of humanity to influence the future. The tendency to freeze the present coincides with a fatalistic perception of change. What we are offered is an interpretation of history that distances men and women from the events that impact on their lives. Human beings are viewed as extraneous to the process of change and therefore are seen as exercising little influence over their destiny. Neither autonomous nor self-determining, individuals are assigned an undistinguished role as objects of history.

People making choices do not need support from bureaucratic institutions. What they require is the freedom to engage with new experience, not just the formal right to choose but cultural support for experimentation and individual choice making. Back in the eighteenth century, the German philosopher Immanuel Kant recognized that it was the emergence of conditions whereby individuals could pursue such activities unimpeded that constituted the point of departure for the Enlightenment. Experimentation and the pursuit of knowledge are not simply good in and of themselves, they also give freedom and democracy real content.

Kant claimed that the 'enlightenment is man's emergence from his self-imposed immaturity'. By immaturity he meant 'the inability to use one's understanding without guidance from another'. According to Kant, this immaturity was self-imposed and its 'cause lies not in lack of understanding, but in lack of resolve and courage to use it without guidance from another'. And confronting his readers with what he characterized as the motto of the Enlightenment – *Sapere Aude* or Dare to Know – he challenged them to use their understanding. Today, when the precautionary principle constantly communicates the prejudice that science threatens to run ahead of society, and that those mounting experiments are 'playing God', daring to know is often represented as an act of irresponsibility. Kant would have been perplexed by contemporary society's uneasy relationship with science and knowledge.

Of course, our ambigious relationship with knowledge and reason is not due to the failure of individual character but the outcome of a more deep-seated process of cultural disorientation. Unfortunately, Kant's diagnosis of self-imposed immaturity is more pertinent to contemporary times than to the circumstances he faced. At a time when the claims of knowledge and science are regarded with mistrust and cynicism, the motto *Sapere Aude* goes against the grain of contemporary cultural sensibility. Yet fortunately, many of us sense that daring to know is what makes us human.

The politics of behaviour represents the conscious negation of the ideal of individual autonomy. To be sure, even at the best of times, individual autonomy is an ideal that can at best be realized inconsistently. People live in a world not of their own making and in circumstances that often elude their aspiration to determine their affairs. The exercise of autonomy has always come up against external constraints – natural obstacles, economic exigencies, wars and conflict, and social dislocation. Today, it also faces a cultural climate that is deeply suspicious of the aspiration for autonomous behaviour.

Human action often results in unexpected outcomes, some of which are uncomfortable to live with. For example, the genetics revolution provides us with important new insights into our constitution but it may also give us information about ourselves that we would rather not know. Nevertheless, the pursuit of the ideal of autonomy offers people the promise of choices and frequently results in progress. It is precisely because some individuals have taken this ideal seriously that they successfully challenge repressive institutions and the use of arbitrary powers that seek to thwart their ambition. We have also learned that the aspiration for autonomy often goes hand in hand with the display of altruism and social solidarity. An enlightened society needs to harness the ideal of individual autonomy to create the optimum conditions for human development. Societies that fail to valorize this ideal end up dominated by a culture of fatalism and risk, collapsing into a state of stasis.

The Enlightenment ideal of individual autonomy insists that society and the state must recognize the independence of each individual. As Bronner argues, 'autonomy originally implied the right for each to have his or her faith'.[1] Such a perspective questions the right of the state to promote a particular faith – be it in the form of a traditional religion or the lifestyle crusades associated with the current policy of behaviour modification. Recognition of the ideal of individual autonomy – an important component of the legacy of the Enlightenment – represents the foundation for choice making, moral and political decision making, and social engagement.

Popular suspicion towards the exercise of human agency

means that the ideal of individual autonomy is frequently dismissed as an illusion fostered by apologists for the free market. It is argued that in a society which is dominated by the media, big corporations and forces unleashed by globalization, individuals lack the capacity for autonomous action. Moreover, as diminished or vulnerable subjects, people do not so much choose their faith as have it foisted on them. That is why the Enlightenment model of the autonomous and responsible citizen is displaced by a more passive disoriented individual who requires the 'support' of public institutions. What we are left with is a regression to the condition of the immature self of the pre-Enlightenment era.

The mood of cultural pessimism does not leave society untouched. It has a profound impact on how people see themselves. It is difficult to *Dare to Know* when our culture continually transmits the signal that risk taking is irresponsible and that caution and safety are the principal virtues of our time. Such signals serve as an invitation to people to constrain their aspirations and limit their actions. If people are repeatedly told that not much is expected of them and that, indeed, they are vulnerable individuals in need of support – they will frequently begin to play the part that is assigned to them. Today, the promise of individual autonomy is contradicted by the reality of a culture that is uncomfortable with its exercise. As a result, individual existence is experienced not so much through the prism of autonomy as of isolation.

The lack of validation accorded to the ideal of autonomy goes hand in hand with a lack of respect for democracy. As we discussed in previous chapters, powerful anti-democratic sentiments have been institutionalized by public bodies that are devoted to treating adults like children. Public policy is frequently inspired by the belief that the electorate cannot be relied on to figure out what is in its best interest. The politics of fear provides one instrument for 'raising the awareness' of people about what's good for them, the politics of behaviour another. Instead of attempting to engage with the public, the oligarchy prefers to offer a diagnosis. So George Lakoff, whose *Don't Think of an Elephant* has been adopted by many liberal Democrats in the US as an explanation of their defeat by George W. Bush, describes those who voted Republican as advocates of authoritarian 'strict-father families' who stress self-interest and greed and competitiveness. These folks hate 'nurturance and care', are religious fanatics, and lack the therapeutic sensibilities of their liberal cousins.[2]

This diagnosis of human inferiority is symptomatic of the anti-democratic attitude of the political oligarchy. In previous times, such contempt for ordinary people was the trademark of the authoritarian right. Today's cultural elite has forgotten that true democrats do not talk about the electorate as if they are mere simpletons who are unaware of their true interests. In the twenty-first century it is not politically correct to refer to people as 'mentally children or barbarians'. Nevertheless, the representation of grown-up citizens as 'vulnerable' people is symptomatic of the profound anti-democratic ethos that we discussed previously.

Humanizing personhood

The version of personhood that is most consistent with the ideals of autonomy, the exercise of choice and history making is that given by the legacy of the Enlightenment. Risk taking, experimentation, the exercise of critical judgement and reason are some of the important attributes of historical thinking and agency. The exercise of these attributes is the precondition for the reconstitution of public life. Through such human activities, people develop an understanding of how purposeful public activity may lead to positive results in the future. Without a sense of agency, personhood lacks the imagination one associates with political engagement. Humanizing personhood requires challenging the prevailing paradigm of vulnerability and gaining acceptance for the humanist concept of personhood (see the boxed section below for a summary of the defining features of each paradigm).

Defining features of the humanist and vulnerability paradigms

Humanist paradigm	Vulnerability paradigm
Valorizes autonomy	Valorizes help-seeking
Orientation towards reasoning	Scepticism towards the efficacy of knowledge
Search for universal values	Affirmation of identity
Positive attitude towards risk taking	Strongly risk-averse
Valuing of experimentation	Celebration of caution and safety
Belief in capacity to change and alter circumstance	Change is perceived as precursor of negative outcome
Oriented towards the future and upholds achievement of the past	Frozen in the present and estranged from the past
Expectation that individuals and communities possess coping skills	Anticipation that individuals/communities are unlikely to cope
Believes that humanity possesses capacity to overcome adversity	Believes that people are defined by their state of vulnerability

The humanist and vulnerability paradigms of personhood never exist in a pure form. Since the rise of the modern era, every culture has internalized elements of both. But cultures nevertheless discriminate when they communicate stories about which forms of behaviour they value and which ones they don't. For example, throughout most of the nineteenth and twentieth centuries the ideals of self-help and self-sufficiency enjoyed cultural affirmation. Today, it is help-seeking that benefits from cultural validation. In contrast to the celebration of risk taking in former times, society today has turned safety into a veritable religion. The ideal of experimentation has been displaced by the conformist embrace of caution, which has been institutionalized through the precautionary principle. The values associated with the humanist paradigm of personhood are not entirely absent but they have become subordinate to ones that promote the sensibility of vulnerability.

Fortunately, human society can never entirely accept the fatalistic dogma of TINA. Nor can it frame its ideal of personhood entirely on the paradigm of vulnerability. That is why sections of society continue to look for a more positive version of this ideal.[3] *Conflicting ideas about the paradigm of personhood are today the equivalent of past clashes of ideologies and political alternatives.*[4] They touch upon such fundamental questions as what it means to be human, the meaning of human nature, and the relationship between the individual and public institutions. Ideas about the paradigm of personhood constitute the point of departure for the formulation of policy and the creation of norms – informal and formal – that regulate people's relationships and individual behaviour. The meaning of personhood has important implications for how we view the relationship of people to history and the potential for changing and altering circumstances. Our attitude towards it informs how we make sense of the exercise of choice and of individual responsibility, and our capacity to know, reason and gain insights into the truth. Ultimately, different ideas about person-hood lead to conflicting ideas about public life. Whether people are perceived as the problem or the solver of problems depends on which paradigm one subscribes to.

In our era of political exhaustion, the challenge that faces us is essentially pre-political. It makes little sense to develop an ambitious political philosophy when the sense of human subjectivity exists in a diminished form. Politics represents the negation of Fate and its existence depends on the prevalence of the belief that what people do can make a difference. That is why today the challenge facing those interested in the reconstitution of public life is not the discovery of a Big Idea or the invention of a new political doctrine or philosophy. In the absence of a more robust sense of human agency that can act on such ideas, such doctrine would have a formal and platitudinous character. Does that not mean abandoning any hope of re-engaging with political life? Not at all, for the most immediate task facing those interested in the recovery of the Enlightenment sensibility towards the future is to contribute to the promotion of the humanist version of personhood. Before politics can be reconstituted we need to foster an intellectual climate that is hospitable to sentiments that directly challenge the prevailing paradigm of vulnerability. Humanizing personhood is the most pressing issue and practical question facing those concerned to challenge the prevailing culture of fatalism.

Aside from the exhaustion of the traditions associated with left and right, there is another reason why we need to stake out a new terrain for the development of public life. With the prevalence of the paradigm of human vulnerability, politics – left or right – has little practical consequence. What matters is whether people are prepared to accept the conformist ethos that freezes society in the present and deprives us of both our past and future. No doubt in the future there may be plenty of doctrinal issues to fight about. But perversely, for now the genuine conservative and liberal and

Socialist have more in common than they suspect. The task of restoring a more human-centred public culture should engage the energies of all those who are inspired by the traditions associated with the historical movement from the Renaissance through to the Enlightenment and twentieth-century modernism. Despite profound political differences, we all have a common interest in rescuing the humanist tradition and reconstructing it in a form appropriate to the twenty-first century.

Progress or fear

The politics of fear thrives on the terrain of misanthropy and cynicism concerning the endeavour of people to alter and improve their circumstances. From this perspective, the instinctive response to such efforts – be they an invention, a new product or an institutional reform – is an expansive sense of suspicion that readily gives way to anxiety and fear. Such attitudes stand ready to write off claims of human progress both in the present and in the past. Indeed, there is a widespread conviction that it is the development of human civilization, particularly the advance of science and technology, and the resulting subordination of the natural order to the demands of human society, that is the source of many of today's problems of environmental destruction and social disintegration. Further developments in the sphere of science and technology tend to be greeted with apprehension rather than celebration. So, for example, recent advances in genetics or nanotechnology are regarded as creating more problems than benefits for society.

Suspicion concerning the possibility of progress means that significant advances in the human condition are regularly reinterpreted as bad news. The very fact that Western society has become concerned about its ageing population reflects the huge progress that has been made in recent years in humanity's struggle against disease. Since 1950 there has been a 17 per cent increase in life expectancy worldwide: this increase has been most spectacular in the poorer nations of Asia, where it has reached 20 per cent. Yet time and again we are told that the struggle to contain disease has been a failure and that we now face new species of plagues and superbugs. Increasingly, we are made to feel as if the risk to our health is greater than before.

Despite Western culture's profound sense of disappointment with the human subject, individuals possess an unprecedented potential for influencing the way they live their lives. It is only now that the promise of choice and control has acquired meaning for a significant section of the public. Autonomy and self-determination are still little more than ideals that can inspire. But we have moved away from the Stone Age of ideologies to a time when the transformative potential of people has acquired a remarkable force. We have also learnt that history does not issue any guarantees. Purposeful change is indeed a risky enterprise. But whether we like it or not, the taking of risks in order to transform our lives and to transform ourselves is one of our most distinct human qualities. The making of history, too, is one of those transformative experiments that help us to realize and define our humanity.

The politics of fear continually produces health warnings about the future. It is hard to be open-minded and forward-looking in an era dominated by caution and the fear of change. But there are many decent people who believe in their humanity and are willing to go against the grain. One step at a time. A worthwhile objective is the cultivation of a second Enlightenment. Some of us are the products of the first, and by trying to engage with the obstacles that have thwarted its realization, we might gain some insights about how to do better the second time around.

The politics of fear thrives in an atmosphere where the exercise of human agency is regarded with suspicion if not dread.

The anti-humanist turn continually blames progress and civilization for every dreadful event from the Holocaust to global warming. It helps fuel the sensibility of the conservatism of fear and its principal virtues of caution and low expectations. The misanthropic worldview of the anti-humanist turn continually communicates the belief that human ambition is a form of greed. The aspiration to greater individual autonomy is decried as selfishness and an insensibility to the sufferings of the vulnerable. From this standpoint, the aspiration to improve the conditions of life – the most basic motive of people throughout the ages and one that has driven humanity from the Dark Ages to civilization – is vilified.

In these conditions we have two choices. We can renounce the distinct human qualities that have helped to transform and humanize the world and resign ourselves to the culture of fatalism that prevails today. Or we can do the opposite. Instead of celebrating passivity and vulnerability we can set about humanizing our existence. Instead of acting as the audience for yet another performance of the politics of fear we can try to alter the conditions that give rise to it.

Notes

Chapter 1

1 Powell (2000), p. 53.
2 See 'Tessa Jowell warns Labour: stop talking bollocks – it scares voters', in the *Scotsman*, 24 December 2004.
3 Hardt and Negri (2000), pp. xii–xiii.
4 Richards (2000), p. 30.
5 O'Hara (2005), p. 117.
6 Anderson (2000), p. 17.
7 Francis Fukuyama (1989), 'The End of History', *The National Interest*, no. 16.
8 'Starbucks to boost fair-trade image', the *Telegraph*, 1 February 2005.
9 'CBI chief claims Davos hijacked by NGOs', the *Guardian*, 31 January 2005.
10 Mair (2000), p. 2.
11 'Flu feared more than terrorist attack', the *Guardian*, 24 January 2005.
12 *BBC News Online*, 24 January 2005.
13 Sontag (1991), pp. 178–9.
14 Watson (2004), p. 8.
15 Bauman (2003), p. 20.
16 See, for example, Peter Berkowitz, 'Enlightenment Rightly Understood', *Policy Review*, no. 128, 2004, p. 1.
17 Lillian Rubin, 'Why Don't They Listen to Us? Speaking to the Working Class', *Dissent Magazine*, Winter 2005, p. 12.

18 Stan Greenberg, cited in Alexander (2005), p. 19.

19 Touraine (2003), p. 310.

20 See Bauman (1998), Beck (2000), Giddens (1999).

21 Bauman (2003), p. 22.

22 Touraine (2003), p. 298.

23 See Reed Jr (2005).

24 See http://pollingreport.com, 'The Latest Trial Heats: Bush/Kerry/ Nader', August 2004.

25 See Fiorina, Abrams and Pope (2004).

26 See survey carried out in Minnesota cited in the Minneapolis *Star Tribune*, 18 September 2004.

27 Jeannette Batz Cooperman, 'Personal Voices: One Country, Two Moralities', *AlterNet*, posted 5 November 2004.

28 Jeannette Batz Cooperman, 'Personal Voices'.

29 Reed Jr. (2005), p. 13.

30 See Steven Kull, *The Separate Realities of Bush and Kerry Supporters* (The University of Maryland: The PIPA/Knowledge Networks Poll), 21 October 2004. This point is further developed by John W. Dean, former counsel to the President, in 'Understanding the 2004 Presidential Election', *Common Dreams News Center*, 13 April 2003.

31 So argues Don Hazen, editor of *AlterNet*, in his introduction to Lakoff (2004), p. xiii.

32 Lakoff (2004), pp. 11–12.

33 Lakoff (2004), pp. 19, 39.

34 Cited in Jonathan Alter's column in *Newsweek*, 15 November 2004.

Chapter 2

1 Dalton (2004), p. vii.

2 Ryan (2004), p. 8.

3 Andreas Schedler, 'Introduction: Antipolitics – Closing and Colonizing the Public Sphere', in Schedler (1997), p. 7.

4 See Mair and Van Biezen (2001).

5 See Seth Gitell, 'Apathy at the polls', *Boston Phoenix*, 4 December 2002.

6 See *The Washington Post*, 14 January 2005.

  7 Mark Weinstein, 'Political Activity and Youth in Britain', in Todd
     and Taylor (eds) (2004), p. 189.
  8 Blais *et al.* (2004), pp. 227–8.
  9 Study by Gary Orren, cited in Skocpol (2003), pp. 245–6.
 10 Mackenzie and Labiner (2002), pp. 2–3.
 11 J. Curtice and R. Jowell, 'The Sceptical Electorate', in Jowell,
     Curtice, Park, Brook and Ahrendt (1995), pp. 141, 148.
 12 Findings of the poll published in the *Guardian*, 8 June 1999.
 13 'Politics a "turn-off" for under 45s', *BBC News*, 28 February 2002.
 14 Huntington (1975), pp. 37–8.
 15 Kaase, Newton and Scanbrough (1997), p. 136.
 16 Dalton (2004), p. 144.
 17 Giddens (1994), p. 17.
 18 Giddens (2001), p. 440.
 19 Norris (2002), p. xi.
 20 Norris (2002), p. 4.
 21 Norris (2002), p. 4.
 22 See Furedi (1999).
 23 Mark Weinstein, 'Political Activity and Youth in Britain', in Todd
     and Taylor (2004), p. 190.
 24 Skocpol (2003), p. 232.
 25 McCullagh (2003), p. 19.
 26 See this argument by Chloe Taylor and others in 'Young's political
     apathy is "a myth"', *The Times Higher Supplement*, 1 April 2005.
 27 Cloonan and Street (1998), p. 35.
 28 Malcolm Todd and Gary Taylor, 'Introduction', in Todd and Taylor
     (2004), p. 22.
 29 O'Toole, Marsh and Jones (2003), p. 358.
 30 See O'Toole, Marsh and Jones (2003).
 31 Dalton (2004), p. 48.
 32 Blais *et al.* (2004).
 33 Norris (2002), p. 8.
 34 Kevin Farnsworth, 'Anti-Globalisation, Anti-Capitalism and the
     Democratic State', in Todd and Taylor (2004), p. 60.
 35 A. Melucci, 'Social Movements and the Democratization of Every-
     day Life', in Keane (1988).

36 Bookchin (1995).
37 Melucci (1989), p. 49.
38 Kingsnorth (2003), p. 83.
39 J. Goodwin, James Jasper and Francesca Polleta, 'Why Emotions Matter', in Goodwin, Jasper and Polleta (2001), p. 9.

Chapter 3

1 Jai Sen, 'Challenging Empires: Reading the World Social Forum', in Sen, Anand, Escobar and Waterman (2004), p. xxiv.
2 Chico Whitaker, 'The WSF as Open Space', in Sen, Anand, Escobar and Waterman (2004), pp. 112, 114.
3 Kingsnorth (2003), p. 231.
4 David Graeber, 'The Globalization Movement and the New New Left', in Aronowitz and Gautney (2003), p. 332.
5 See *Der Spiegel*, 21 February 2005, p. 24.
6 Giddens (1994), p. 9 and Gray (1995), p. 93.
7 Weltman (2003), p. 244.
8 *New Statesman*, 24 September 2004.
9 See Howard Kurtz, 'Writer backing Bush Plan had gotten federal contract', *Washington Post*, 26 January 2005.
10 Giddens (1994), pp. 78–9.
11 Bauman (2003), p. 22.
12 Bell (1980), p. 149.
13 Piccone (1999), p. 7.
14 Aron (1978), p. 228.
15 William H. McNeill, 'Winds of Change', *Foreign Affairs*, Fall 1990, p. 161.
16 Adam Meyerson, 'The Vision Thing, Continued', *The Policy Review*, Summer 1990, p. 2.
17 Himmelfarb (2001).
18 O'Hara (2005), pp. 113–14.
19 Norbert Lechner, 'Politics in Retreat: Redrawing Our Political Maps', in Schedler (1997), p. 179.
20 See Blaine Harden, 'The Greening of Evangelicals', *Washington Post*, 6 February 2005.

21 Norbert Lechner, 'Politics in Retreat', p. 179.
22 Giddens (1994), p. 49.
23 Norbert Lechner, 'Politics in Retreat', p. 179.
24 Bronner (2004), p. 2.
25 Jürgen Habermas, 'Popular Sovereignty as Procedure', in Bohman and Rehg (1999), p. 37.
26 Mouzelis (2001), p. 447.
27 'For struggles, global and national – Samir Amin interviewed by V. Sridhar', in Sen, Anand, Escobar and Waterman (2004), pp. 7–8.
28 Bennett (2004), p. 2.
29 Bronner (2004), p. 1.
30 Barry (2001), p. 9.
31 Bobbio (1996), p. 47.
32 Bobbio (1996), p. 5.
33 Harris (2005), p. 163.
34 Polly Toynbee, 'New Labour gives you no chance to vote for a vision', the *Guardian*, 2 March 2005.

Chapter 4

1 'Individuals increasingly expect greater personal autonomy and are as a result less subservient to authority', notes a major study commissioned by the British Government. See Performance and Innovation Unit, *Social Capital: A Discussion Paper*, April 2002, p. 43.
2 O'Toole, Marsh and Jones (2003), p. 238.
3 See Furedi (2004), *Therapy Culture: Cultivating Vulnerability in an Anxious Age*, chapter 5.
4 See Furedi (2004), *Therapy Culture: Cultivating Vulnerability in an Anxious Age*.
5 Frankenberg, Robinson and Delahooke (2000), pp. 588–9.
6 See the *Guardian*, 2 April 2005.
7 Frankenberg, Robinson and Delahooke (2000), pp. 588–9.
8 Beck (1992), p. 49.
9 See Furedi (1992), pp. 204–9.

10 'Introduction' to Alexander and Sztompka (1990), p. 24.
11 See Furedi (2004), *Therapy Culture: Cultivating Vulnerability in an Anxious Age*, chapter 2 for a discussion of this issue.
12 Luhmann (1993), p. 44.
13 Peter Knight, 'ILOVEYOU: Viruses, Paranoia and the Environment of Risk', in Parish and Parker (2001), p. 21.
14 Melley (2000), p. vii.
15 Timothy Melley, 'Agency Panic and the Culture of Conspiracy', in Parish and Parker (2001), p. 62.

Chapter 5

1 This rumour is reported in *Zaman Daily*, 9 January 2005. The threat of an asteroid-caused tsunami was raised by Galen Gisler, a Los Alamos National Laboratory scientist. See *ABQjournal*, 11 January 2005.
2 Bernhard Giesen, 'The Trauma of Perpetrators', in Alexander, Eyerman, Giesen, Smelser and Sztompka (2004), p. 146.
3 Piotr Sztompka, 'The Trauma of Social Change', in Alexander, Eyerman, Giesen, Smelser and Sztompka (2004), p. 164.
4 Norbert Lechner, 'Politics in Retreat: Redrawing Our Political Maps', in Schedler (1997), p. 179.
5 Vico (1961), pp. 52–3.
6 Hayek (1978), p. 31.
7 Terry Eagleton, 'Where do postmodernists come from?', in Wood and Foster (1997), p. 24.
8 *Planet Ark*, 10 July 2002.
9 Broswimmer (2002).
10 Diamond (2004).
11 Cited by Mick Hume, 'The vacuous irrelevant hunting debate sums up British politics', *The Times*, 6 September 2004.

Chapter 6

1 Frank (2004), p. 248.
2 Alexander (2005).

3 Wallis (2005).
4 Frank (2004), p. 1.
5 Bennett (2003), p. 17.
6 Alexander (2005), p. 6.
7 William Davies, 'Will the secular left continue bowling alone?', *New Statesman*, 15 November 2004.
8 Michael Gronewalter, 'Don't get Smart, get Stupid', *DemocraticUnderground.Com*, 24 April 2002.
9 http://www.yubanet.com/cgi-bin/artman/exec/view.cgi/10/14328, 14 October 2004.
10 Gary Indiana, 'No Such Thing as Paranoia', *The Village Voice*, 25 May 2004.
11 Moore (2001), p. 87.
12 Bauman (2003), p. 20.
13 Dalton (2004), p. 91.
14 Furedi (2004), p. 89.
15 Baker (2002), p. 926.
16 Archibugi (2004), p. 440.
17 Archibugi (2004), p. 452.
18 Zum (2004), p. 10.
19 Zum (2004), p. 10.
20 Malcolm J. Todd and Gary Taylor, 'Introduction', in Todd and Taylor (2004), p. 25.
21 Kevin Farnsworth, 'Anti-Globalisation, Anti-Capitalism and the Democratic State', in Todd and Taylor (2004), p. 61.
22 See Skocpol (2003).
23 Skocpol (2003), p. 151.
24 Skocpol (2003), p. 224, 228–9.
25 John Vidal, 'Seeds of Dissent', the *Guardian*, 17 August 1999.
26 Cherny (2000).
27 See G. Monbiot, 'Disruptive protest is a civic duty', the *Guardian*, 19 August 1999.
28 Skopcol (2003), p. 11.
29 Gorg and Hirsch (1998), p. 598.
30 Pimbert and Wakeford (2001), p. 23.
31 Smith and Wales (2000), p. 55.

32 Smith and Wales (2000), p. 52.

33 Smith and Wales (2000), p. 60.

34 See Thompson and Hoggett (2000), p. 352, and Hoggett and Thompson (2002), p. 120.

35 Pinbert and Wakeford (2001), p. 23.

36 Gregg Martin, 'New Social Movements and Democracy', in Todd and Taylor (2004), p. 37.

Chapter 7

1 See Todd May, 'Religion, the Election and the Politics of Fear', *countercurrents.org*, 19 November 2004.

2 Don Hazen, 'Grappling with the Politics of Fear', *AlterNet*, 9 March 2005.

3 'Blunkett bails out crime at top of the agenda', the *Guardian*, 24 November 2004.

4 Cited in Paul Linford, 'Tony Blair turns to the politics of fear', *The Journal*, 27 November 2004.

5 See 'Politics of Fear Stalks Britain', *Yahoo News*, 28 February 2005.

6 'Attacks on Tory politics of fear', the *Guardian*, 1 April 2005.

7 Ashton Carter, John Deutch and Philip Zelikow, 'Catastrophic Terrorism: Tackling the New Danger', *Foreign Affairs*, November/December 1998, p. 81.

8 See *BBC Online*, 2 September 2001.

9 Jim VandeHei and Howard Kurtz, *Washington Post*, 29 September 2004.

10 Giroux (2003), p. 13.

11 'The Monster at the Door', *Common Dreams News Centre*, 30 September 2004.

12 See Michael Fitzpatrick, 'Fearing Flu', www.spiked-online.com, 27 January 2005.

13 Cited in Robin (2004), p. 11.

14 Cited in Heartfield (2002), p. 195.

15 Heartfield (2002), p. 195.

16 See *The Yorkshire Post*, 11 March 2005.

17 Don Hazen, 'Grappling With the Politics of Fear'.
18 Shklar (1989), pp. 23, 29, 30.
19 Robin (2004), p. 129.
20 Jeffrey C. Alexander, 'On the Construction of Moral Universals', in
    Alexander, Eyerman, Giesen, Smelser and Sztompka (2004), pp. 246,
    252, 263.
21 Beck (2002), p. 46.
22 Giddens (1994), p. 20.
23 Giddens (1994), p. 223.
24 Michael Walzer, 'All God's Children Got Values', *Dissent Magazine*,
    Spring 2005, pp. 3–6.
25 Marcus (2002), pp. 103–4.
26 Mark Lawson, 'Icebergs and Rocks of the "Good" Lie', the
    Guardian, 24 June 1996.
27 Cited in Dick Taverne, 'Careless science costs lives', the *Guardian*,
    18 February 2005.
28 'It's a hell of a town', the *Guardian*, 19 May 2005.
29 Robin (2004), p. 135.
30 Robin (2004), p. 139.
31 Cited in Filler (2003), p. 345.

Chapter 8

1 Department of Health (2005), *Choosing a Better Diet: A Food and
   Health Action Plan*, p. 7. (London: Department of Health).
2 See 'Remarks by the President and the First Lady at the White House
   Conference on Teenagers: Raising Responsible and Resourceful
   Youth', White House Office of the Press Secretary, 2 May 2000.
3 Dorothy S. Strickland, 'The Role of Parents and Grandparents in
   Children's Cognitive Development: Focus on Language and Literacy', White House Summit on Early Childhood Cognitive
   Development, 27 July 2001.
4 'Children at centre of drive for a fitter nation', the *Guardian*, 10
   March 2005.
5 Paul Barker, 'Lovers of freedom should fear for Britain, not the US',
   the *Guardian*, 10 January 2005.

6 Home Office, *Supporting Families: A Consultation Document*, p. 30, 1998, London.

7 'Draft Speech for the Home Secretary – Launch of the Lords and Commons Family and Child Protection Group's Report "Family Matters"', 23 July 1998.

8 See 'Police target domestic violence', *The Times*, 16 March 1995.

9 Cited in ' "Nanny state" minister under fire', *BBC News-online*, 26 November 2004.

10 Department of Health (2005), *Choosing Activity: A Physical Activity Plan* (London: Department of Health), p. 11.

11 Cited in 'Public wants a "nanny state" ', *BBC News-online*, 28 June 2004.

12 See Tessa Jowell, 'Politics of Behaviour', the *Observer*, 21 November 2004.

13 Cited in Michael White, 'Frank Field plan to beat yobs', the *Guardian*, 10 December 2004.

14 Cited in Flint (2004), p. 2.

15 For Field's usage of the term see Field (2003).

16 Giddens (1994), p. 156.

17 Lasch (1979), p. 43.

18 See P. Hoggett, 'Agency, Rationality and Social Policy', in Lewis, Gewirtz and Clarke (2000), p. 144.

19 See Williams (1998), pp. 132–3.

20 See Paul Hoggett, 'Social Policy and the Emotions', in Lewis *et al.* (2000), p. 145.

21 Richard Layard, 'Happiness is Back', *Prospect*, March 2005, issue 108.

22 Cited in Furedi (2004), *Therapy Culture: Cultivating Vulnerability in an Anxious Age*, p. 49.

23 Frank E. Scott, 'Reconsidering a therapeutic role for the state: anti-modernist governance and the reunification of the self', http://online.sfsu.edu/~fscott/scottf2000apsa.htm, 2000, p. 8.

24 For a discussion of the therapeutic state see Nolan (1998) and Furedi (2004), *Therapy Culture: Cultivating Vulnerability in an Anxious Age*, chapter 8.

25 Arnason (2000), p. 194.

26 Pupavac (2001), p. 3.

27 Department of Health (2005), pp. 7, 22.

28 Piccone (2002), p. 149.

29 Orwell (1949), p. 216.

30 'Artists win change to Bill outlawing religious hatred', *The Times*, 7 February 2005.

31 Mick Hume, 'Questioning the New Conformism', *Spiked-online*, 4 March 2005.

Conclusion

1 Bronner (2004), p. 136.

2 Lakoff (2004).

3 As I write this chapter I am delighted to discover that a group of swimmers won a legal battle to bathe outdoors without the presence of lifeguards in a lake on London's Hampstead Heath. See 'Hardy bathers win right to swim unsupervised', the *Guardian*, 27 April 2005.

4 These conflicts underpin some of the clashes of the so-called Culture Wars.

Bibliography

Alexander, D. (2005), *Telling It Like It Could Be: The Moral Force of Progressive Politics* (London: The Smith Institute).

Alexander, J. C. (2001), 'Robust Utopias and Civil Repairs', *International Sociology*, vol. 16, no. 4.

Alexander, J. C. and Sztompka, P. (eds) (1990), *Rethinking Progress* (Boston: Unwin Hyman).

Alexander, J. C., Eyerman, R., Giesen, B., Smelsar, N. L. and Sztompka, P. (2004), *Cultural Trauma and Collective Identity* (Berkeley: University of California Press).

Anderson, P. (2000), 'Renewals', *New Left Review* 2/1, January/February 2000.

Archibugi, D. (2004), 'Cosmopolitan Democracy and its Critics: A Review', *European Journal of International Relations*, vol. 10, no. 3.

Arnason, A. (2000) 'Biography, Bereavement Story', *Mortality*, vol. 5, no. 2.

Aron, R. (1978), *Politics and History* (New York: The Free Press).

Aronowitz, S. and Gautney, H. (2003) (eds), *Implicating Empire: Globalization and Resistance In the 21st Century World Order* (New York: Basic Books).

Axford, B. and Huggins, R. (1998) 'Anti-politics or the Triumph of Postmodern Populism in Promotional Cultures?', *Telematics and Informatics* 15.

Bahnisch, M. (2003) 'Social Change at the End of History? Theorising the Exhaustion of the Modern Political Imaginary and the Hauntology of Late Modern Politics', paper presented to the Social Change in the 21st Century Conference (Centre for Social Change Research, Queensland University of Technology).

Baker, G. (2002), 'Problems in the Theorisation of Global Civil Society',

Political Studies, vol. 50.

Barry, B. (2001), *Culture and Equality: An Egalitarian Critique of Multiculturalism* (Cambridge: Polity).

Bauman, Z. (1993), *Postmodern Ethics* (Oxford: Blackwell).

Bauman, Z. (1998), *Globalization: The Human Consequences* (Cambridge: Polity).

Bauman, Z. (2003), 'Utopia with Topos', *History of the Human Sciences*, vol. 16, no. 1.

Beck U. (1992), *Risk Society: Towards a New Modernity* (London: Sage).

Beck, U. (2000), *What is Globalization?* (Cambridge: Polity).

Beck, U. (2002), 'The Cosmopolitan Society and its Enemies', *Theory, Culture & Society*, vol. 19 (1–2).

Beck, U. and Beck-Gernsheim, E. (2002), *Individualization* (London: Sage).

Bell, D. (1980), *Sociological Journeys: Essays 1960–1980* (London: Heinemann).

Bennett, W. L. (2003), 'New Media Power: The Internet and Global Activism', in N. Couldry and J. Curran, (eds) *Contesting Media Power* (New York: Rowman and Littlefield).

Bennett, W. L. (2004), 'Branded Political Communication: Lifestyle Politics, Logo Campaigns, and the Rise of Global Citizenship', in M. Micheletti, A. Follesdal and D. Stolle, (eds), *The Politics Behind Products* (New Brunswick, NJ: Transaction Books).

Berlin, I. (1991), 'The Decline of Utopian Ideas in the West', in *The Crooked Timber of Humanity* (London: Fontana).

Blais, A., Gidengil, E., Nevitte, N. and Nadeau, R. (2004), 'Where does Turnout Decline Come From?', *European Journal of Political Research*, vol. 43.

Blaug, R. (2002), 'Engineering Democracy', *Political Studies*, vol. 50.

Bobbio, N. (1996), *Left and Right: The Significance of a Political Distinction* (Cambridge: Polity Press).

Bohman, J. (1999), 'Survey Article: The Coming of Age of Deliberative Democracy', *The Journal of Political Philosophy*, vol. 6, no. 4.

Bohman, J. and Rehg, W. (eds) (1999), *Deliberative Democracy: Essays on Reason and Politics* (Cambridge, MA: MIT Press).

Bookchin, M. (1995), *Social Anarchism or Lifestyle Anarchism: An*

Unbridgeable Chasm (San Francisco: AK Press).

Bronner, S. E. (2004), *Reclaiming The Enlightenment: Toward A Politics of Radical Engagement* (New York: Columbia University Press).

Broswimmer, F. J. (2002), *Ecocide: A Short History of the Mass Extinction of Species* (London: Pluto Press).

Canovan, M. (1999), 'Trust the People! Populism and the Two Faces of Democracy', *Political Studies*, vol. xlvii.

Cherny, A. (2000), *The Future of Public Life in the Information Age* (New York: Basic Books).

Cloonan, M. and Street, J. (1998), 'Rock the Vote: Popular Culture and Politics', *Politics*, vol. 18, no. 1.

Creveld, van M. (1999), *The Rise and Decline of the State* (Cambridge: Cambridge University Press).

Dalton, R. J. (2004), *Democratic Challenges, Democratic Choices: The Erosion of Political Support in Advanced Industrial Democracies* (Oxford: Oxford University Press).

Department of Health (2005), *Delivering Choosing Health: Making Healthier Choices Easier* (London: Department of Health Publications).

Diamond, J. (2004), *Collapse: How Societies Choose to Fail or Survive* (London: Allan Lane).

The Electoral Commission (2004), *An Audit of Political Engagement*, www.electoralcommission.org.uk.

Ferreira, J. (1990), 'Cultural Conservatism and Mass Culture', *Journal of American Culture*, vol. 13, no. 1.

Field, F. (2003), *Neighbours from Hell: The Politics of Behaviour* (London: Politico's).

Filler, D. M. (2003), 'Terrorism, Panic and Pedophilia', *Virginia Journal of Social Policy & the Law*, Spring 2003.

Fiorina, M. P., Abrams, S. and Pope, J. (2004), *Culture War? The Myth of a Polarized America* (New York: Longman Publishing Group).

Fishkin, J. (1992), 'Talk of the Tube: How to Get Teledemocracy Right', *The American Prospect*, Fall (11).

Flint, J. (2004), 'The Responsible Tenant: Housing Governance & the Politics of Behaviour', CNR Paper 20: August 2004, ESRC Centre for Neighbourhood Research.

Frank, T. (2004), *What's The Matter With America? The Resistible Rise of the American Right* (London: Secker & Warburg).

Frankenberg, R., Robinson, I. and Delahooke, A. (2000), 'Countering Essentialism in Behavioural Social Science: The Example of the "Vulnerable Child" Ethnographically Examined', *The Sociological Review*, vol. 38, no. 2.

Furedi, F. (1992), *Mythical Past, Elusive Future: History and Society in an Anxious Age* (London: Pluto Press).

Furedi, F. (1999), *Counting Mistrust: The Hidden Growth of a Culture of Litigation in Britain* (London: Centre for Policy Studies).

Furedi, F. (2004), *Therapy Culture: Cultivating Vulnerability in an Anxious Age* (London: Routledge).

Furedi, F. (2004), *Where Have All the Intellectuals Gone?: Confronting 21st Century Philistinism* (London: Continuum).

Furedi, F. (2005, originally published 1997), *Culture of Fear: Risk Taking and the Morality of Low Expectation* (London: Continuum).

Gane, N. (2001), 'Chasing the "Runaway World": The Politics of Recent Globalization Theory', *Acta Sociologica*, vol. 44.

Giddens, A. (1992), *Modernity and Self-Identity* (Cambridge: Polity).

Giddens, A. (1994), *Beyond Left and Right: The Future of Radical Politics* (Stanford: Stanford University Press).

Giddens, A. (1998), *The Third Way: The New Renewal of Social Democracy* (Cambridge: Polity Press).

Giddens, A. (1999), *Runaway World: How Globalization is Reshaping Our Lives* (London: Profile Books).

Giddens, A. (2001), *Sociology* (4th edn; Cambridge: Polity Press).

Giroux, H. A. (2003), *The Abandoned Generation: Democracy Beyond the Culture of Fear* (New York: Palgrave Macmillan).

Goodwin, J., Jasper, J. M. and Polleta, F. (eds) (2001), *Passionate Politics: Emotions and Social Movements* (Chicago: The University of Chicago Press).

Gorg, C. and Hirsch, J. (1998), 'Is International Democracy Possible?', *Review of International Political Economy*, vol. 5, no. 4.

Gottfried, P. (2002), *Multiculturalism and the Politics of Guilt* (Columbia: University of Missouri Press).

Gray, J. (1995), *Enlightenment's Wake: Politics and Culture at the Close of the Modern Age* (London: Routledge).

Hale, S., Leggett, W. and Martell, L. (eds) (2004), *The Third Way and Beyond: Criticisms, Futures, Alternatives* (Manchester: Manchester University Press).

Hall, P. (1999), 'Social Capital in Britain', *British Journal of Political Science*, vol. 29, no. 3.

Hardt, M. and Negri, A. (2000), *Empire* (Cambridge, MA: Harvard University Press).

Harris, J. (2005), *So Now Who Do We Vote For?* (London: Faber & Faber).

Hayek, F. (1978), *Three Sources of Human Values* (London: LSE).

Heartfield, J. (2002), *The 'Death of The Subject' Explained* (Sheffield: Sheffield Hallam University Press).

Heartfield, J. (2003), 'Postmodern Desertions: Capitalism and Anti-Capitalism', *Interventions*, vol. 5, no. 2.

Henn, M., Weinstein, M. and Wring, D. (1999), *Young People and Citizenship: A Study of Opinion in Nottinghamshire* (Nottingham: Nottinghamshire County Council).

Himmelfarb, G. (2001), *One Nation: Two Cultures* (New York: Vintage).

Himmelfarb, G. (2004), *The Roads to Modernity: The British, French, and American Enlightenments* (New York: Alfred A. Knopf).

Hoggett, P. and Thompson, S. (2002), 'Toward a Democracy of Emotions, *Constellations*, vol. 9, no. 1.

Huntington, S. (1975), 'The Democratic Distemper', *Public Interest*, 41.

Jacoby, R. (1999), *The End of Utopia: Politics and Culture in an Age of Apathy* (New York: Basic Books).

Jowell, R., Curtice, J., Park, A., Brook, L. and Arendt, D. (eds) (1995), *British Social Attitudes: the 12th Report* (Dartmouth: SCPR).

Kaase, M., Newton, K. and Scanbrough, K. (1997), 'Beliefs in Government', *Politics*, vol. 17, no. 2.

Kalb, J. (2002), 'Understanding Conservatism and Tradition', *Telos*, Winter 2002, no. 122.

Keane, J. (ed.) (1988), *Civil Society and the State* (London: Verso).

Kingsnorth, P. (2003), *One No, Many Yeses: A Journey to the Heart of the Global Resistance Movement* (London: Free Press).

186   **Bibliography**

Lakoff, S. (2004), *Don't Think of an Elephant: Know Your Values and Frame the Debate (A Progressive Guide to Action)* (White River Jct., Vermont: Chelsea Green Publishing).

Lasch, C. (1979), *The Culture of Narcissism: American Life in an Age of Diminishing Expectations* (New York: Warner Books).

Lewis, G., Gewirtz, S. and Clarke, J. (eds) (2000), *Rethinking Social Policy* (London: Sage Publications).

Luhmann, N. (1993), *Risk: A Sociological Theory* (New York: Walter de Gruyter).

Mackenzie, G. and Labiner, J. (2002), *Opportunity Lost: The Decline of Trust and Confidence in Government After September 11* (Washington DC: Center for Public Services).

Mair, P. (2000), 'Populist Democracy vs Party Democracy', presentation to the ECPR Workshop on Competing Conceptions of Democracy, University of Copenhagen, 14–19 November 2000.

Mair, P. and Van Biezen, I. (2001), 'Party Membership in Twenty European Democracies 1980–2000', in *Party Politics* (London: Sage Publications).

Marcus, G. (2002), *The Sentimental Citizen: Emotion in Democratic Politics* (University Park, Penn: The Pennsylvania State University Press).

McCullagh, K. (2003), 'E-democracy: Potential for Political Revolution?', *International Journal of Law and Information Technology*, vol. 11, no. 2.

Melley, T. (2000), *Empire of Conspiracy: The Culture of Paranoia in Postwar America* (Ithaca: Cornell University Press).

Melucci, A. (1989), *Nomads of the Present: Social Movements and Individual Needs in Contemporary Society* (London: Hutchinson Radius).

Micheletti, M. (2000), 'Shopping and the Reinvention of Democracy: Green Consumerism and the Accumulation of Social Capital in Sweden', paper for the ECPR Joint Sessions 2000 Workshop, Copenhagen, Denmark, 14–19 April.

Moore, M. (2001), *Stupid White Men ... and Other Sorry Excuses for the State of the Nation!* (New York: Regan Books).

Mouzelis, N. (2001), 'Reflexive Modernization and the Third Way: The

Impasse of Giddens' Social-democratic Politics', *The Sociologial Review*, vol. 50, no. 3.

Mudde, C. (2004), 'The Populist Zeitgeist', *Government and Opposition*, vol. 39, issue 4.

Nolan, J. L. (1998), *The Therapeutic State: Justifying Government at Century's End* (New York: New York University Press).

Norris, P. (2002), *Democratic Phoenix: Reinventing Political Activism* (Cambridge: Cambridge University Press).

O'Hara, K. (2005), *After Blair: Conservatism Beyond Thatcher* (Cambridge: Icon Books).

Orwell, G. (1949), *Nineteen Eighty-Four* (London: Secker and Warburg).

O'Toole, T., Marsh, D. and Jones, S. (2003), 'Political Literacy Cuts Both Ways: The Politics of Non-participation among Young People', *The Political Quarterly*, vol. 74, no. 3.

Parish, J. and Parker, M. (eds) (2001), *The Age of Anxiety: Conspiracy Theory and the Human Sciences* (Oxford: Blackwell Publishers).

Park, A. (1998), *Young People's Social Attitudes 1998: Full Report of Research Activities and Results* (Keele: ESRC).

Parkinson, J. (2003), 'Legitimacy Problems in Deliberative Democracy', *Political Studies*, vol. 51, no. 4.

Piccone, O. (2002), 'From the New Left to Postmodern Populism: An Interview with Paul Piccone', *Telos*, no. 132.

Piccone, P. (1999), '21st Century Politics', *Telos*, Fall, no. 117.

Pimbert, M. and Wakeford, T. (2001), 'Overview – Deliberative Democracy and Citizen Empowerement', *PLA Notes* 40, February.

Powell, M. (2000), 'New Labour and the Third Way in the British Welfare State: A New And Distinctive Approach?', *Critical Social Policy*, no. 62.

Pupavac, V. (2001), 'Therapeutic Governance: Psychosocial Intervention and Trauma Risk Management', unpublished paper, London.

Purdy, J. (1999), *For Common Things: Irony, Trust, and Commitment in America Today* (New York: Alfred A. Knopf).

Reed Jr, A. (2005), 'The 2004 Election in Perspective: The Myth of "Cultural Divide" and the Triumph of Neoliberal Ideology', *American Quarterly*, vol. 57, no. 1.

Reich, R. B. (2004), *Reason: Why Liberals Will Win the Battle for America* (New York: Alfred A. Knopf).

Richards, P. (2000), *Is the Party Over? New Labour and the Politics of Participation* (London: Fabian Society).

Robin, C. (2004), *Fear: The History of a Political Idea* (Oxford: Oxford University Press).

Rose, N. (2001), 'The Politics of Life Itself', *Theory, Culture & Society*, vol. 18, no. 6.

Rosenblum, N. L. (1989) (ed.), *Liberalism and the Moral Life* (Cambridge, MA: Harvard University Press).

Roth, P. (2001), *The Human Stain* (London: Vintage).

Ryan, M. (2004), 'Red Tops, Populists and the Irresistible Rise of the Public Voice. (2)', *Journal for Crime, Conflict and the Media*, vol. 1, no. 3.

Schedler, A. (ed.) (1997), *The End of Politics? Explorations Into Modern Antipolitics* (Houndmills: Macmillan Press).

Sen, J., Anand, A., Escobar, A. and Waterman, P. (2004), *The World Social Forum: Challenging Empires* (New Delhi: Viveka). Available in pdf format at www.choike.org/neuvo_eng/informes/1557.html.

Shklar, J. N. (1989), 'The Liberalism of Fear' in Rosenblum, N. (ed.), *Liberalism and the Moral Life* (Cambridge, MA: Harvard University Press).

Skocpol, T. (2003), *Diminishing Democracy – From Membership to Management in American Civic Life* (Norman: University of Oklahoma Press).

Smith, G. and Wales, C. (2000), 'Citizens' Juries and Deliberative Democracy', *Political Studies*, vol. 48.

Sontag, S. (1991), *AIDS and its Metaphors* (London: Penguin).

Taggart, P. A. (1996), *The New Populism and the New Politics: New Protest Parties in Sweden in a Comparative Perspective* (London: Macmillan).

Taguieff, P. (1995), 'Political Science Confronts Populism: From a Conceptual Mirage to a Real Problem', *Telos*, no. 103.

Thomas, J., Jewell, J. and Cushion, S. (2003), 'Stirring Up Apathy? The Media and the 2003 Welsh Assembly elections', paper presented at 'Can Vote, Won't Vote Conference', Goldsmiths College, London, 6 November 2003.

Thompson, S. and Hoggett, P. (2000), 'The Emotional Dynamics of Deliberative Democracy', *Policy & Politics*, vol. 29, no. 3.

Todd, M. J. and Taylor, G. (eds) (2004), *Democracy and Participation: Popular Protest and New Social Movements* (London: Merlin Press).

Touraine, A. (1995), *Critique of Modernity* (Oxford: Blackwell).

Touraine, A. (2003), 'Meaningless Politics', *Constellations*, vol. 10, no. 3.

Turner, C. (2003), 'Manheim's Utopia Today', *History of the Human Sciences*, vol. 16, no. 1.

Vico, G. (1961), *The New Science* (New York: Anchor Paperback).

Wallis, J. (2005) *God's Politics: Why the Right Gets It Wrong and the Left Doesn't Get It* (New York: HarperSanFrancisco).

Watson, D. (2004), *Death Sentence: The Decay of Public Language* (Sydney: Vintage).

Weltman, D. (2003), 'From Political Landscape to Political Timescape: The Third Way and the Ideological Imagining of Political Change and Continuity', *Time and Society*, vol. 12, no. 2/3.

Weltman, D. and Billig, M. (2001), 'The Political Psychology of Contemporary Anti-Politics: A Discursive Approach to the End-of-Ideology Era', *Political Psychology* vol. 22, no. 2.

White, C., Bruce, S. and Ritchie, J. (2000), *Young People's Politics: Political Interest and Engagement amongst 14–24 Year Olds* (York: Joseph Rowntree Foundation).

White, S. (ed.) (2001), *New Labour: The Progressive Future?* (Houndmills, Hampshire: Palgrave).

Williams, S. J. (1998), ' "Capitalising" on Emotions? Rethinking the Inequalities in Health Debate', *Sociology*, vol. 32, no. 1.

Wood, E. M. and Foster, J. B. (eds) (1997), *In Defense of History: Marxism and the Postmodern Agenda* (New York: Monthly Review Press).

Young, I. M. (2001), 'Activist Challenges to Deliberative Democracy', *Political Theory*, vol. 29, no. 5.

Zum, M. (2004), 'Global Governance and Legitimacy Problems', *Government and Opposition*, vol. 39, no. 2.

Index